Religious
Language
and
Knowledge

RELIGIOUS LANGUAGE AND KNOWLEDGE

Edited by
Robert H. Ayers and
William T. Blackstone

University of Georgia Press
Athens

Library of Congress Catalog Card Number: 72–169950
International Standard Book Number: 0–8203–0269–4

The University of Georgia Press, Athens 30601

Printed in the United States of America
by Heritage Printers, Inc.
Charlotte, North Carolina 28202

CONTENTS

INTRODUCTION

Our age has been characterized as an age of atheism and scepticism, and there is some truth to this claim. Traditional religion has been undermined by the Marxian perspective that religion is the opiate of the masses, by the Freudian view that God is the projection of a father image on the universe, by atheistic existentialism and humanism, and by the "death of God" theology.

Perhaps the strongest challenge, however, has come from philosophers of the logical empiricist and analytic schools. These philosophers question not merely the truth of the key claims of religion but the very meaningfulness of those claims. The logical empiricist consigns theological claims to the garbage heap of linguistic nonsense on the grounds that those claims do not meet his verifiability test. The philosophical analyst, whose theory of meaning and linguistic cupboards are not so rigid as those of the positivist, does not write off religion so readily. He finds religious discourse to be meaningful, but frequently, in agreement with the positivist, characterizes the linguistic functions or meanings of that discourse as non-assertive or non-cognitive. Thus, even the broadened theory of meaning of the philosophical analyst constitutes a severe challenge to religion. For if no religious utterances have cognitive meaning, the non-cognitive uses or functions of religious discourse which are emphasized by the analyst lose much of their traditional significance. It makes little sense to exclaim, "Praise be to Thee, O God," if nothing of a cognitive nature can be said about God.

The essays in this volume, all of which were originally presented in the 1965 Great Thinkers Forum sponsored by the Department of Philosophy and Religion at the University of Georgia, explore this contemporary challenge to religion. A variety of positions are taken, but all of the essays are united in their concern with the meaning of religious language and the problem of religious knowledge.

Five of the essays deal specifically with the question of the cognitive status of religious utterances. Viewing the problem from both the perspective of the falsifiability criterion and the "meaning is use" approach, Blackstone comes to a rather sceptical conclusion. Broiles explicates some of the difficulties found in R. N. Hare's "blik" theory of religion and argues against this non-descriptivist account. Professors Clarke and Harrison, after describing the challenge presented to religion by linguistic philosophy, argue that at least the basic religions claim, "there is a God," is assertive. They argue that this statement is a logically necessary one and that it asserts a necessary state of affairs. This position, if viable, negates the force of much of the verifiability or falsifiability challenge. Nielsen, on the other hand, argues straightforwardly for the atheist position. On any interpretation of the claim that God exists which is factually significant, he declares, it is a false claim.

Hartshorne rehabilitates some of the classical arguments for the existence of God and indicates what logical price must be paid for denying the reality of God, while Ayers analyzes the place of mythical language in religion, arguing that mythical language need not be seen as irrational if certain standards of judgment are employed. In the one essay which deals with the epistemology of religious thought outside the western tradition, Altizer discusses the dialectical methodology of Buddhism and compares it with the Hegelian dialectic. This essay makes clear the basic foundation for much of Altizer's "death of God" theology.

All of these essays make valuable contributions toward the understanding and resolution of the contemporary challenge to theology and religion.

Robert H. Ayers
W. T. Blackstone

NOTES ON CONTRIBUTORS

W. T. Blackstone is Professor of Philosophy, Head of the Department of Philosophy and Religion, and Chairman of the Division of Social Sciences at the University of Georgia. He is the author of a number of articles in philosophical journals and of several books, including *The Problem of Religious Knowledge* and *Francis Hutcheson and Contemporary Ethical Theory.*

Kai Nielsen was formerly Professor of Philosophy at New York University and is currently Research Professor of Philosophy at the University of Calgary. A prolific writer, Professor Nielsen has contributed numerous essays to leading philosophical and theological journals and is author of a forthcoming book, *The Quest for God.*

Bowman L. Clarke is Professor of Philosophy and Coordinator of Graduate Studies in Philosophy at the University of Georgia. He is a frequent contributor to leading philosophical and theological journals and is the author of *Logic and Natural Theology.*

Charles Hartshorne is Professor of Philosophy at the University of Texas. A world-renowned process philosopher, Professor Hartshorne has been a Fulbright Professor at Melbourne University and the Perry Lecturer at Yale University. Author of many essays in philosophical journals, his books include *Reality and Social Process, Philosophy and Psychology of Sensation, Man's Vision of God, The Divine Relativity,* and *The Logic of Perfection.*

Robert H. Ayers is Professor of Religion at the University of Georgia. He has contributed a number of articles to theological journals.

Thomas J. J. Altizer was formerly Associate Professor of Bible and Religion at Emory University and is presently Professor of Religion at the State University of New York at Stony Brook. Known as a leading exponent of the "death of God" theology, Altizer is the author of *Oriental Mysticism and Biblical Eschatology, Mircea Eliade and the Dialectic of the Sacred*, and *Christian Atheism*.

Frank R. Harrison III is Associate Professor of Philosophy at the University of Georgia. He has contributed articles to several philosophical journals and is the author of *Deductive Logic and Descriptive Language*.

R. David Broiles was formerly Assistant Professor of Philosophy at the University of Georgia. He is the author of *The Moral Philosophy of David Hume*.

THE STATUS OF GOD-TALK*

William T. Blackstone

I will begin by telling a story or a parable which was originally told by Professor Wisdom and which is here paraphrased by Professor Flew:

> Once upon a time two explorers came upon a clearing in the jungle. In the clearing were growing many flowers and many weeds. One explorer says, "Some gardener must tend this plot." The other disagrees, "There is no gardener." So they pitch their tents and set a watch. No gardener is ever seen. "But perhaps he is an invisible gardener." So they set up a barbed-wire fence. They patrol it with bloodhounds. (For they remember how H. G. Wells' *The Invisible Man* could be both smelt and touched though he could not be seen.) But no shrieks ever suggest that some intruder has received a shock. No movements of the wire ever betray an invisible climber. The bloodhounds never give cry. Yet still the Believer is not convinced. "But there is a gardener, invisible, intangible, insensible to electric shocks, a gardener who has no scent and makes no sound, a gardener who comes secretly to look after the garden which he loves." At last the Sceptic despairs, "But what remains of your original assertion? Just how does what you call an invisible, intangible, eternally elusive gardener differ from an imaginary gardener or even from no gardener at all?"[1]

The moral of this story is obvious. The assertion, "There is a gardener," has become so qualified that we can no longer understand what, if anything, is being asserted. In the same manner, the statement, "God exists," or other religious claims can "die the death of a thousand qualifications," to use Flew's phrase. They can be so qualified that they are compatible with any conceivable empirical state of affairs. But being compatible with

*This essay appeared in somewhat different form as "The Status of God-Talk," *Journal for the Scientific Study of Religion* 5 (Fall 1966): 357–365.

any state of affairs and incompatible with none, they no longer seem to say anything. If, on the other hand, some conceivable state of affairs, for example, the existence of "needless suffering" counts against, say, the existence of God, then, at least to some extent, the meaning of the statement "God exists" is made clear.

The implicit test here for empirical significance has become known as the falsifiability test. To my knowledge, it was first clearly formulated by Karl Popper. Popper says that "the empirical content of a statement increases with its degree of falsifiability: The more a statement forbids, the more it says about the world of experience."[2] If it forbids nothing, it has no empirical content. Popper is careful to state that this test is not a test of meaningfulness in general but is only a criterion of demarcation, which enables us to distinguish statements which belong in the area of empirical science from metaphysical statements, logic, and mathematics. Quite clearly, he intended it as a test of empirical significance and this test has become the central motif of the contemporary "Theology and Falsification" discussion.[3] As a test, it seems to me to be a very mild one, especially when compared to those formulated in the early stages of the development of logical positivism. Actually, I see little difference between this falsifiability test and the milder "confirmability" test of the later Carnap.[4] The demand that there must be a way of falsifying a proposition is similar to the demand that there must be a way of confirming it, for the proposition which (if true) confirms another proposition will (if false) falsify it.[5] Whether this test is called the falsifiability test or the confirmability test or the verifiability test makes little difference. We will be utilizing this test in this paper.

As indicated in the parable above, a number of contemporary philosophers have been puzzled by the apparently non-falsifiable status of religious claims. They are puzzled because, although it is a sociological fact that many people think they are making ordinary factual claims in their God-talk, it is a logical fact that such talk does not behave like ordinary factual discourse. They have been led, then, to ask the following questions: How are we to characterize religious beliefs? What is their logical status? Do such beliefs have factual significance? Do they obey the rules for propositions? Or is the content of religious beliefs inexpressible in propositional form? Are religious beliefs "no more than a series of sounds obeying no rules and like the babblings of an idiot, full of sound and fury, signifying nothing?"[6] If religious beliefs do not obey the rules of propositions, then do they obey other rules and hence have a meaning or logical status or structure uniquely their own?

These, then, are the questions confronting religion today, more specifically, the philosopher of religion. His problem might be characterized as meta-theological, that of ascertaining the status and structure of theological-religious claims, and is a problem parallel to that confronting the moral philosopher, the meta-ethical problem of the elucidation of the status and structure of moral discourse.

Responses to these questions have been many and varied, ranging from Hare's characterization of religious beliefs as "bliks"[7] to Braithwaite's theory that they are disguised moral judgments[8] to Hick's account of them as eschatological predictions.[9] Some of these theories have been "outrageously simplistic." Some have been sceptical, others not. Those who have been led to a kind of scepticism by their puzzlement are sceptics, however, in an entirely different sense from that of the traditional religious sceptic. The traditional sceptic doubted that religious beliefs could be proven or could even be shown to be probable. The contemporary sceptic doubts that religious beliefs are significant factual claims. He doubts that they are even intelligible possibilities for belief. His scepticism, then, is at a more fundamental level than that of the traditional sceptic, for he calls into question not the truth but the meaningfulness of religious claims.

Much of contemporary Anglo-Saxon philosophy stresses that in order to discover the logic or structure of any discourse, including religious discourse, we are obliged to examine that discourse in the context of its use and function. Wittgenstein's impact on contemporary analytic philosophy has been exactly this—to make clear that language has many uses and purposes, that the logic of one use of language, the rules governing the symbols of that use, might be quite different from the rules governing the symbols in another use of language or type of discourse.[10] There is no single test of meaningfulness such as some contended the verifiability principle was. It may well be that religious discourse does not obey the rules of scientific discourse. This does not mean that it has *no* meaning, no significance. It may well obey other kinds of rules, have a different kind of structure, a different kind of use and function, and hence a different kind of significance. It is the task of the philosopher of religion to attempt to specify that structure or use.

True, some of the early positivists had a particularly narrow, self-stultifying test for meaningfulness and they overstated their case against religion when they stated that it was nonsense. Crombie correctly speaks of Ayer as a wolf "who would devour as meaningless all theological statements in one meal."[11] Significance in general certainly includes much more than factual significance. However, it seems to me that the positivists were on the right track in developing a test for empirical significance. If such a test can be satisfactorily devised, then the application of it can tell us something we want to know, namely whether certain sentences, religious in this case, have empirical significance. If such sentences do not meet this test, we cannot infer that they are nonsense. They may have another use or function or another kind of significance. But if they do not meet the test, then something important, though negative, is discovered and we are led to see important and fundamental differences between religious discourse and other kinds of discourse.

Not all religious discourse gives rise to philosophical perplexities. Without raising the question of the criteria necessary to make a belief a religious one, it seems clear that the class of religious sentences includes commands, exhortations, blessings, questions, ejaculations, descriptions, explanations, historical statements, autobiographical statements, etc. Most of these are not perplexing at all. The symbols in these sentences obey certain rules of language and have a reasonably clear-cut use and structure. Certain religious claims, however, are really quite perplexing. Although on the surface they appear to be ordinary descriptive claims, they do not behave logically as ordinary descriptive claims. I have in mind certain uses of the following claims: "God exists," "God loves us," "God is our heavenly father," and "Jesus is the son of God."

What I propose to do in this paper is examine and talk about some of these philosophically perplexing religious statements. I delimit my concern and the conclusions of my analysis to these claims in western Christianity. Although my conclusions may well apply to statements in the framework of other of the world's major religions, I do not want to make that claim here.

Let me say right off that I do not pretend to have *the* answer to this question. If there is any lesson to be learned from contemporary philosophy, it is to be extremely suspicious of any wholesale defense or critique of areas or types of discourse. We need more piece meal analyses rather than sweeping ones. This does not preclude a general appraisal of an area of discourse. It is simply to insist that such an appraisal be based on specific and careful analysis.

Before proceeding, let me make it quite clear that one frequent response to the problem of the significance of religious-theological language simply will not do. That response is that religion is a matter of faith, not of proof. One finds this response in many theologians, including Tertullian, Pascal, Kierkegaard, and Barth. Is it not quite clear, however, that one first must be aware of the content of a belief or set of beliefs before the question of the acceptance of that belief or set of beliefs on faith or other grounds can even arise? If I say to you "Cumquats gurnalate elactically, accept this on faith," surely the first question that enters your mind is: What in the world did he say? What is the meaning of that string of words? So too in regard to religious beliefs. Before the question of acceptance on faith of beliefs such as "God exists" or "Christ is the son of God" can arise, the meaning of these claims must be made clear to some extent. If we are unable to understand what the word "God" means or what it would be like for the sentence "God exists" to be true or false, if we are unable to specify some conceivable state of affairs or set of conditions which would verify or falsify this sentence, then the request that we accept the existence of God on faith is parallel to the request that we accept "Cumquats gurnalate elactically" on faith.

Our point is that the problem of the significance of religious claims is logically prior to the issue of accepting those claims on faith or other grounds. This is true even if the notion of religious faith includes, as it surely does, much more than the acceptance of certain beliefs. Furthermore, to maintain, as some do, that religious beliefs are significant and true to God, even though from our finite perspective we can neither grasp their significance nor establish their truth, is of no succor and in fact leaves us in a position where communication may become impossible, whether this is viewed as communication between believer and God or between religious believers. What this position commits us to is the notion of a language in which certain words in that language possess a meaning which is beyond the comprehension of every user of that language.[12] Even if God knows the meaning of "God exists," this does not make this sentence intelligible in human discourse.

The first thing we might note is that religious concepts, and statements in which they occur, have a number of uses and functions. The sentence "God exists," for example, is often used to express attitudes, to persuade actions, to threaten, to make factual claims, etc. We are specifically interested in its use as a factual claim. And quite clearly most Christian believers do take this sentence and others, like "God loves us," to be making claims about the world. But are such statements empirical claims? Are such statements verifiable or falsifiable in principle? It seems to me that the answer to this question depends upon the kind of "believer" involved. There is a class of believers, characterized by some as the garden variety type, who maintain that God is an entity, a being, different from the ordinary objects of our experience, but an entity to which our ordinary predicates apply in a descriptive manner. Traditional anthropomorphites fall into this class. Kierkegaard seems to have such believers in mind when he ironically speaks of those who would conceive of God much like "the figure of a very rare and tremendously large bird, with a red beak, sitting in a tree on the mound, and perhaps even whistling in an unheard-of manner."[13] To such believers, Kierkegaard claims, "The divine is simply a rhetorically meaningless hiatic superlative of the human: which explains their satisfaction with the idea of being able to form ever clearer conceptions of it."[14]

Although such garden variety believers may have what some call an improper concept of God or a concept of a being who is not an adequate object of the religious attitude or worship, nonetheless, from the point of view of a philosophical analyst, some very definite things can be said in their favor. Their religious claims, as straightforward empirical claims, and the symbols used in them, obey the rules for propositions. They also conform to the falsifiability test. That is, there is no serious problem with their meaning status. The problem for the anthropomorphite is the truth-status of his claims. There seems to be little evidence for his beliefs.

None of the great theologians have been believers of the garden variety, however. These theologians have insisted that our ordinary predicates cannot be applied to God without qualification, that the symbols in religious statements do not obey the ordinary rules of language. Symbols in religious statements enable us to "see in a glass darkly." They provide us with "models," "analogies," "stories," "pictures," "parables," or "images," and these are presumed to give us some religious insight, some insight into God's nature; but none of these stories, parables, images, or analogies which constitute theological statements are to be construed as literal truths. Nor are these statements (without semantic loss) translatable into literal statements, into statements, for example, about the natural order. They remain always semantically opaque. In fact, this is an *essential* characteristic of such discourse, for it is not about an ordinary identifiable particular. Although the symbol "God" resembles in its use a proper name like "John," it differs from ordinary proper names in that its use is not based on acquaintance with the being it denotes. God is transcendent, beyond our experience and comprehension; he is "pure being," "the ground of being," "the ground of the universe," the "mysterium tremendum," the "wholly other," the "unconditioned transcendent." Tillich, speaking of religious symbols, says that "They must express an object that by its very nature transcends every object in the world that is split into subjectivity and objectivity. A real symbol points to an object which can never become an object. Religious symbols represent the transcendent but do not make the transcendent immanent. They do not make God a part of the empirical world."[15] God, Tillich says, does not exist; that is, he does not exist in the sense in which ordinary objects exist. God is beyond all differentiations which distinguish ordinary objects from one another. He cannot be directly characterized in any way. Only the statement that " 'God is being itself' is a non-symbolic statement . . . after this has been said, nothing else can be said about God which is not symbolic. . . . Therefore, if anything beyond this bare assertion is said about God, it is no longer a direct and proper statement, no longer a concept. It is indirect, and it points to something beyond itself. In a word, it is symbolic."[16]

I must confess that I have difficulty with the meaning of this one non-symbolic statement which Tillich permits. However, the difficulty I wish to stress concerns symbolic talk about God and, although I have picked on Tillich, it is a difficulty which applies to other theologians as well. Professor Alston puts my difficulty succinctly: "since we can say nothing non-symbolically about being itself, a given symbol cannot be judged in terms of the reality or unreality of that aspect of being itself which it is being used to symbolize."[17] The same point is made by Coburn: "apart from some independent information about what it is that is being metaphorically described, not the remotest clue is provided by such statements as to the respects in which the thing referred to by "God" is asserted (or implied) to resemble the things to which the general term which purports to fulfill the descriptive role in the utterance literally applies."[18] The point is that any terms which are used metaphorically, symbolically, or analogically to describe or characterize an object (in this case, God) can fulfill this function only if we have some literal, non-symbolic, non-analogical descriptive knowledge about that object. Suppose we use the notion of a shepherd as a symbol of God. On what grounds can we judge that this symbol is appropriate unless we independently know something literal about God, namely, that he providentially cares for his children?[19] Furthermore, the symbol or analogue communicates something to us only if this literal knowledge is presupposed. Again, suppose, in speaking of God, we say: "God is a person," or "God is personal."[20] Now the general assumption is not that God is literally a person, that he literally has the characteristics which persons have. We use the notion of "person" or "personal" as a symbol or analogue. But if we have no literal descriptive knowledge of God, how could we ever know whether this symbol is appropriate, and even assuming that it is, how could we ever have any ideas of the manner in which God resembles a person, and the manner in which he does not? It seems to me that without some straightforward literal knowledge of God, we cannot, and it is for this reason that the appeal to symbolic meaning and analogical predication fails. Even talk about the incarnated moral characteristics of Christ does not help in conveying to us information about God as transcendent, unlimited being.[21]

What, then, is communicated by theological talk? Do theologians simply provide us with "a night in which all cows are black," with discourse in which the symbols obey no rhyme or reason or any rules, with statements which are compatible with any state of affairs, with statements which lack criteria for their application, and which do not have connected with them any set of conditions which would settle the question of their truth or falsity?

It seems that one cannot go so far as to say that theological talk has no rhyme or reason, that it obeys no rules at all. One can say, however, and with the blessings of many of the theologians themselves, that theological talk does not obey the rules of ordinary discourse about empirical objects. Some theologians, however, want to have their cake and eat it too. They want to maintain that religious discourse does not obey the rules of propositions or straightforward empirical claims and yet that such language communicates factual data, correctly at that, about the world. God is not like Santa Claus or the Easter Bunny[22] and our religious statements are not about mere imaginary or conceived referents. Clearly, however, the theologian, in order to substantiate his claim, must specify the rules governing the symbols in his claims. If, as he claims, theological statements need not possess the ordinary criteria as a necessary condition of those statements having empirical sense; if he claims that such sentences have empirical significance even though they do not have connected with them sets of conditions which would settle the question of the truth or falsity of those sentences, then the burden of proof lies with the theologian to show this. Later, I will suggest a way of interpreting some key theological statements which attempts to make sense of their peculiarities.

Let me briefly analyze one more key religious claim in Christianity: "Christ is the son of God," the doctrine of the Incarnation. I choose this belief because it constitutes perhaps the key belief in Christianity, one which St. Paul characterized as a stumbling block to Jews and foolishness to Greeks. This doctrine has provided the flame for the most heated theological controversies, and yet, it is not clear what is being asserted, if anything, by the statement. The theologian Tertullian straightforwardly stated that this belief is paradoxical and incomprehensible but insisted that, although absurd and impossible, it was to be believed anyhow. Emil Brunner follows the same line. "The hallmark of logical inconsistency," he claims, "clings to all genuine pronouncements of faith."[23] "The natural man takes offence" at these religious claims, for "they are mysteries in which God reveals Himself as the Incomprehensible."[24] Speaking specifically of the Incarnation, Brunner remarks that it is "the entrance into history of that which, by its very name, cannot enter into history, because it is eternal."[25] This claim is "incurably paradoxical." It is self-contradictory to assert that that which is eternal and cannot enter into history does in fact enter into history. Kierkegaard speaks of this same belief as an "absolute paradox." Although paradoxical, the belief that "God has come into being, has been born, grown up, and so forth"[26] must be accepted by Christians.

What, then, is the problem with this theological stand on the doctrine of Incarnation? The problem is this: quite clearly, these theologians maintain that the Incarnation doctrine performs an informative function, and yet, at the same time, it is clear that the doctrine, as "incurably paradoxical," violates a fundamental requirement for using language informatively. That requirement is that a statement be internally consistent. Statements of the form, "X is the case and X is not the case," or statements in which one applies incompatible predicates to the same thing at the same time, do not impart information or communicate facts. "Contradicting oneself is like writing something down and then erasing it, or putting a line through it. A contradiction cancels itself and leaves nothing."[27]

Now if the Incarnation doctrine only *appears* to be paradoxical, if it can be reformulated in non-paradoxical form, then this problem disappears. For example, the statement, "Whoever would save his life would lose it," seems to be contradictory because, ordinarily, the term "save" contradicts what is meant by "lose." But a non-paradoxical, meaningful, and informative translation or interpretation of that sentence is that preoccupation with one's own life to the exclusion of others results in one's losing the ethical character of one's life.[28] Such a translation of the Incarnation doctrine, by their own admission, is precluded by these theologians, for this belief is an absolute, incurable paradox. It is, of course, understandable that the "natural man" takes offense at such a belief. Most of us cannot emulate the example of the White Queen who could believe "three impossible things before breakfast."

It seems to me that the reply of Brunner, that the philosopher or one who insists upon the requirement of internal consistency and complete reliance upon reason is guilty of the sin of pride, is complete hogwash. That God wants us to believe self-contradictions, even assuming that it makes sense to do so, is peculiar indeed. As one philosopher puts it, "It is no light thing to speak in the name of God, and, when the message is unintelligible, the philosopher shrewdly suspects that this unintelligibility is an indication, not of its divine origin, but of the muddleheadedness of the theologians who concocted it."[29]

In spite of Tertullian, Brunner, and Kierkegaard, I do not want to completely rule out a non-paradoxical interpretation of the Incarnation doctrine—although the most recent attempt to do this and retain the fact-stating function of the doctrine seems to me a complete failure.[30] If such an interpretation cannot be made, then the Christian believer, who is urged to accept or believe the Incarnation doctrine, is in a peculiar position indeed. For how can he believe a statement which is self-contradictory? The issue of the acceptance of this doctrine on faith, or that of proving it to be true cannot possibly arise, for it is a logically impossible state of affairs and necessarily false, given the syntactical and semantical rules of our language.

Is one justified in concluding that the doctrine is meaningless? I think not. In fact, one may well learn a great deal from Tertullian, Brunner, and Kierkegaard without being led to their conclusion. If the doctrine cannot be sensibly interpreted along literal lines, then perhaps its use and function is not that of stating an empirical fact or even a logically necessary one. Although its surface-grammar *is* that of a straightforward factual claim, perhaps its real function, its hidden function is normative, not descriptive. Perhaps the function of the claim "Christ is the son of God" is that of recommending a certain way of life, a certain set of attitudes, and a certain pattern of behavior. It might be read: "You ought to live the kind of life espoused by Christ." It seems to me that this statement has at least this function, the function of expressing and evoking emotion and commitment to a set of values. It has been the banner for great social revolutions and movements for centuries.

Of course, statements can perform more than one logical function. Could not this claim fulfill both this normative function and a descriptive one? Believers, I feel confident, will insist that it does. But if they are unable to elucidate this descriptive component, if they are unable to even formulate the statement so that it is internally consistent, if they are unable to specify any set of conditions which would either verify or falsify the claim, then one is led to the conclusion that the statement is nondescriptive.

Let us take an example from non-religious discourse to reinforce this point. I borrow this example from Professor Nielsen.[31] Suppose someone claims that "modern man is alienated." Now this statement can be used and is sometimes used to make a straightforward empirical claim. It might be used to say that many modern men have no interest or pride in their work. They performs jobs merely to make money. They receive no sense of accomplishment and satisfaction and their life is one of pointless drudgery. They are uprooted and have no sense of belonging. If this is what the sentence claims, then, it is reasonably clear and generates no philosophical perplexity.

Suppose, however, someone says, "Modern man is alienated," and like the theologian Paul Tillich, goes on to say that this alienation is "inescapable," that it "follows from the structure of the universe." Man, Tillich says, in his existential situation inevitably experiences "estrangement from his true being." There is the anxiety of emptiness and doubt. Now, is Tillich's claim some kind of empirical generalization about man's psychology or his social environment? To some extent his statement functions in this way. But he seems to want to claim more than this. Man's alienation is inevitable. It is not merely a contingent fact, something that happens to him. Nor do we find Tillich treating this claim as an empirical hypothesis. He does not accumulate case histories of men and gather statistics. What, then, is the function of the statement, "Man is alienated"? Is it a logically true statement, a statement true in virtue of the rules of language, like "All unmarried men are bachelors"? Tillich, I think, would not be happy with this suggestion. But what alternative can he offer? If the claim is not logically true, if it does not function as an empirical generalization, that is, if the question of the falsifiability or testability of the claim by reference to contingent states of affairs is irrelevant, then it might be profitable to view it as a non-descriptive claim, perhaps a disguised value judgment, a surreptitious device to recommend a certain pattern of conduct.

I am suggesting, then, that the logical behavior of certain statements in religious discourse and other areas of discourse, as opposed to the "surface grammar" of those statements, leads us toward a non-descriptive account of those statements. Statements about God in particular, in the context of many of their uses, seem to function as expressions of the value commitments of their users and as devices to recommend those values and it is profitable to view them in this way. This meta-linguistic thesis I am not proposing as a dogma, but as a hypothesis which has prima facie plausibility. Its plausibility rests on the grounds that it has explanatory power. It explains at least *some* of the logical behavior of these sentences.

I am not suggesting, however, the complete assimilation of religious discourse to moral discourse. This would be much too simple. Bishop Butler was surely correct in his assertion that "everything is what it is and not another thing." We have learned much from this significant tautology in the area of moral discourse, and if we heed Butler's advice, we shall not straightforwardly and without qualification reduce religious discourse to some other kind. Undoubtedly, religious discourse has certain uses and functions which are *uniquely* its own. These should be clearly portrayed in a philosophical analysis of that discourse. This can be done by portraying the affinities and resemblances which religious discourse has to moral discourse and to other types of discourse, and it can be done in an illuminating way, without reducing religious discourse to some other kind.

Professor Ferre, in a recent and perceptive analysis, has taken a long step in this direction.[32] He has characterized a number of uses and functions of religious discourse. Conative-emotive functions which he lists include the ceremonial function, in which the speaker uses language to associate himself with the believing community; the liturgical function, a use of language in the act of worship which helps to bring about certain attitudes; the ethical function, a use of language in which one expresses the determination to live a certain kind of life; the judging function, a use which evokes and expresses emotions of unworthiness, guilt, and moral inadequacy, and others.

There is no question that religious discourse has all of these functions. None of them, however, are cognitive uses of language, i.e., make claims about reality. This cognitive function, this fact-stating, fact-claiming function of religion is what we have been specifically interested in in this paper. This function, it seems to me, is the most important function of that discourse. It is so for this reason: the conative-emotive functions mentioned above make sense and are appropriate only if a backdrop of factual belief is presupposed. And yet, if our suggested analysis is correct, it is just this fact-stating function which key religious statements fail to provide.

Our conclusion, then, is a rather sceptical one. Although religious discourse is meaningful in a number of senses, i.e., it has a multiplicity of uses and functions, certain key statements in that discourse, which are purportedly fact-stating and non-anthropomorphic, do not conform to the falsifiability or confirmability test. We must conclude that they lack empirical significance. Our analysis leaves open the possibility that they are assertive in another sense, namely, that they assert logically necessary states of affairs. My colleague, Professor Bowman Clarke, suggests this possibility with one key religious claim, "God exists."[33] In effect, Professor Clarke challenges the "contemporary view" that logically true propositions merely assert something about our uses of words. Such propositions assert necessary facts, some non-contingent facts about the world. Hence the falsifiability test is not an adequate test of all factual significance. He agrees that necessary propositions are shown to be true or false on the basis of syntactical and semantical rules alone. But it does not follow that such propositions are about words and not about the world. They are about the world. They are about states of affairs which are non-contingent, which could not be otherwise. The proposition, "God exists," asserts such a state of affairs. It will be interesting to see Professor Clarke's suggestion worked out in some detail. Especially for those who accept the "contemporary outlook," there are difficulties with the notion of a necessary fact or necessary state of affairs. But the logically true status of "God exists" surely accounts for much of the logical behavior of that statement in religious-theological discourse, specifically for the fact that, in many of its uses, no contingent state of affairs could ever falsify the statement. A choice between alternative meta-theological analyses must be made, it seems to me, on the basis of which one has the greatest explanatory power, which one best accounts for the logical behavior of religious statements.

I have in this paper been talking about language and some might suggest that our concern and conclusions are "purely academic." If this phrase means that they concern only academicians and have no relevance to the lives of human beings, let me assure you that this is not the case. My conclusions have definite implications for the religious life, in this case specifically for the Christian. Let me indicate certain logical implications by uttering a tautology. If statements like "God loves us," "God is angry at sin," "Christ is the son of God" are pseudo-factual claims and function non-descriptively, perhaps as expressions of value commitments and as recommendations of a set of values, then it makes no sense to accept or believe those claims as empirically significant claims. And yet it seems clear that the traditional Christian did take and the contemporary Christian still takes these statements to be empirically significant claims. If my suggested conclusions are correct, this becomes logically impossible. Such "beliefs" are irrational because they are not even intelligible possibilities for belief. A possible causal consequence of our analysis is this: If our demythologized version of these key religious sentences is accepted, that is, if the believer becomes convinced of the non-descriptive status of his beliefs, then it may well be that those beliefs will not have the impact on his life that they had when viewed as descriptive truths. To indicate the logical implications and possible causal consequences of our analysis of religious discourse is not, of course, to make a value judgment about religion. It is not to say that we should do away with religion, that religion has no importance. Quite the contrary, religion is of vast importance. As an attempt to formulate a framework of total orientation for one's life, it is surely the most crucial and the most precious of all human concerns. Our concern here is not to deprecate religion but to become clear about the meaning status of religious claims.

Notes

1. Antony Flew, "Theology and Falsification," *New Essays in Philosophical Theology*, eds. Antony Flew and Alasdair MacIntyre (New York: The Macmillan Company, 1955), p. 96.

2. Karl Popper, *The Logic of Scientific Explanation* (New York: Basic Books, 1959), p. 119; originally published in German in 1931 as *Logik der Forschung*.

3. See Flew, MacIntyre, and Basil Mitchell, eds., *Faith and Logic* (London: George Allen and Unwin, 1957).

4. Rudolf Carnap, "Testability and Meaning," *Philosophy of Science* 3 (1936) and 4 (1937).

5. See John Passmore, "Logical Positivism (1)," *The Australasian Journal of Philosophy* 21 (1943): 87.

6. Bowman Clarke, "Linguistic Analysis and the Philosophy of Religion," *The Monist* 47 (1963): 373.

7. R. M. Hare, "Theology and Falsification," in Flew and MacIntyre, *New Essays*.

8. R. B. Braithwaite, *An Empiricist View of the Nature of Religious Belief* (Cambridge: Cambridge University Press, 1955).

9. John Hick, *Faith and Knowledge* (Ithaca, New York: Cornell University Press, 1957).

10. See Ludwig Wittgenstein, *Philosophical Investigations* (Oxford: Basil Blackwell and Mott, 1953), English translation by G. E. M. Anscombe.

11. I. M. Crombie, "The Possibility of Theological Statements," in Basil Mitchell, *Faith and Logic*, p. 77.

12. Professor Robert Coburn, in "The Hiddenness of God and Some Barmecidal God Surrogates," *The Journal of Philosophy* 57 (1960): 698–699, elucidates some of the absurdities of this notion: "(1) It would be possible for two statements in the language in question to be in fact equipollent (or contradictory) without anybody's knowing (or even suspecting) that this was so . . . . (2) It would be possible that certain statements constructible in the language in question should be true (false) without anybody's having any idea what would show (or even count for) the truth (falsity) of these statements . . . . (3) It would be possible that every speaker of the language in question should have a certain belief, even though not one of them should understand what it is they all believe to be the case."

13. *Kierkegaard's Concluding Unscientific Postscript*, trans. David E. Swenson (Princeton: Princeton University Press, 1944), p. 219.

14. *The Journals of Kierkegaard*, trans. Alexander Dru (New York: Harper Torchbooks, 1958), p. 172.

15. Paul Tillich, "The Religious Symbol," *Religious Experience and Truth*, ed. Sidney Hook (New York: New York University Press, 1961), p. 303.

16. Paul Tillich, *Systematic Theology* (London: Nisbet and Co., 1953), 1, pp. 264–265.

17. William P. Alston, "Tillich's Conception of a Religious Symbol," in Hook, *Religious Experience*, p. 18.

18. Coburn, *Journal of Philosophy*, p. 702.

19. Alston, in Hook, *Religious Experience*, p. 17.

20. See Coburn's discussion of this, p. 702.

21. See William T. Blackstone, *The Problem of Religious Knowledge* (Englewood Cliffs: Prentice-Hall, 1963), pp. 114–115.

22. See Kai Nielsen, "On Speaking of God," *Theoria* 28 (1962): 126.

23. H. Emil Brunner, *Philosophy of Religion from the Standpoint of Protestant Theology*, 2d ed. (London: James Clarke and Co., 1958), p. 55.

24. Ibid., p. 96.

25. Emil Brunner, *The Mediator, a Study of the Central Doctrine of the Christian Faith* (Philadelphia: Westminster Press, 1947), p. 107.

26. *Concluding Unscientific Postscript*, p. 188.

27. P. F. Strawson, *Introduction to Logical Theory* (London, 1952), p. 3.

28. B. F. Kimpel, *Language and Religion* (New York: Philosophical Library, Inc., 1957), p. 113.

29. Robert Leet Patterson, "Universal Religion and Special Revelation," *The Review of Religion* 10 (1945): 353.

30. Professor Larsen concludes that although the Incarnation is only an apparent paradox, "we cannot draw a distinction which resolves the apparent contradiction." (Robert E. Larsen, "Kierkegaard's Absolute Paradox," *Journal of Religion*, 42, 1962, 41.) However, if we cannot draw distinctions which resolve the contradiction, then it seems that the contradiction is real, not apparent. To treat the Incarnation as a unique fact which cannot be described in a straightforward way but can only be pointed at by using language which is self-contradictory, is no help, involving as it does the peculiar notion of an inexpressible or unstatable fact. See Robert Coburn's discussion of this notion in "The Hiddenness of God and Some Barmecidal God Surrogates," *The Journal of Philosophy* 57 (1960): 704–705.

31. Nielsen, pp. 123–125.

32. Frederick Ferre, " 'Believing That' and the Dimensions of Faith" in K. Bendall and F. Ferre, *Exploring the Logic of Faith* (New York: Association Press, 1962), pp. 43–76.

33. See Bowman Clarke, "Linguistic Analysis and the Philosophy of Religion," *The Monist* 47 (1963).

RELIGION AND COMMITMENT

Kai Nielsen

The end of ideology has been proclaimed. Whether or not it will come to an end is hard to predict. We do not know whether with our present understanding of ideology intellectuals will finally cease making claims that in reality are only empty rhetorical flourishes but are intended by their authors and taken by some of their hearers—hearers taken in by the ideology—to be grand cosmological claims about the nature and destiny of man.[1] But it is plain enough that a *philosopher ought not* as a philosopher to be an ideologist. Many think that philosophy, as conceptual analysis, should place itself quite modestly with the rest of the academic disciplines and renounce all claim to giving us reasoned insight into the human condition. Philosophers should not even seek to discover certain general principles, as Aristotle, Descartes and Hegel did, but they should limit themselves to conceptual analysis or, if you will, pure description of those fundamental concepts that perplex us. It is often maintained that it is *not* a philosopher's job to propose general theses, to discover general principles, and above all it most certainly is not his job to be a sage or an ideologist. That is to say, it is not his job to tell his fellowman what his nature and destiny is or give him a blueprint of the good life. Any such attempt would be both absurd and un-believably pretentious; his proper scholarly niche is to clear up the confusions that arise when we do not properly understand the workings of our language in certain very crucial areas, e.g., in talk about "time," "good," "God," "cause," "freedom," "truth," and the like.

Now I am ambivalent about this. I most certainly do not want, as a philosopher, to be an ideologist and I don't want other philosophers to be ideologists either. Ever since I was a graduate student, I have been distressed at the hollowness and the ideological character of traditional philosophers' talk about the nature and destiny of man. Much of what they have said about the nature of the good life has seemed to me ideological—empty obscurantist rhetoric passed off as statements of general principles about the ultimate nature of reality. Philosophers from Plato to Royce, and even down to such obscurantist mystagogues as Heidegger and Tillich, have indeed upon occasion said penetrating things about life. But, as John Passmore has perceptively noted, exactly the same thing can be found in the great novelists and dramatists.[2] The difference presumably is that the philosopher, unlike the sage, has *thought through* his principles; he doesn't *simply rely on insight* but also upon argument and reason. He doesn't seek simply to be perceptive but to give grounds for his insights. But the arguments one finds such philosophers using to support their insights are very obscure and often incoherent, and the metaphysical machinery is not infrequently scarcely intelligible. Increasingly with philosophers such as Heidegger, Sartre, and Jaspers, one gets what is in effect a contempt for closely reasoned argument. They dish out the dark, yet sometimes insightful sayings and you can either take them or leave them. They are not to be argued about and no serious attempt is made to reason for them. I expect what attracts nonphilosophers to Plato, Spinoza, or Sartre is not their towering metaphysical systems but their sage remarks about life. The strictly philosophical superstructure is not understood by them, but they feel that in some way—which they as neophytes do not understand—these philosophers' insights are supported by their obscure metaphysical superstructures and that people with a thorough training in philosophy can and do, if they are wise and deep men, understand this obscure talk and that perhaps they too could come to understand it, if only they would study it hard enough and long enough. But if even a little bit of what we have learned from analytic or linguistic philosophy is correct, these philosophical superstructures are in Wittgenstein's celebrated phrase "houses of cards." Such philosophy is ideology and a good philosopher should expose it for what it is, e.g., he should show how disguised nonsense is patent nonsense.

Rightly or wrongly, I believe that this low estimate of the metaphysical claims and systematizings of much of traditional philosophy and contemporary continental philosophy is on the whole just. Yet, as I have said, I am ambivalent, for while I want nothing of such metaphysics or such philosophical systems, I am also unhappy with just doing analysis, *if* this somehow is taken to *deny* that the *end* of a philosopher's activity should be to give insight into the problems of life, though most certainly insight supported by argument. I very much feel the force of Austin's remark that we don't yet have enough clarity in philosophy and that it will be time enough to say that clarity is not enough *in philosophy* when we have achieved a tolerable degree of that. But I remain obstinately concerned with the question "*Clarity for what?*" and, like Wittgenstein, I am concerned to "assemble reminders for a particular purpose." I remain, if I dare put it so naively, concerned with trying to understand the concept of truth and the concept of knowledge; and I find I am interested in them because I am vitally interested in trying to know what, if anything, it is possible to know about what sort of life a man ought to lead, what would be a good life and what would be an ideal society; and I very much want to know what, if anything, this has to do with God, freedom and immortality. My activities as a philosopher center around this enterprise, but I most certainly do not want to be simply a sage, simply an undisciplined, free-floating intellectual, journalist or publicist and most certainly I do not want simply to be an ideologist. But I am prepared to argue for philosophical theses, though I am not concerned to construct a philosophical system; but as a philosopher I am concerned with the soundness of these theses and the necessity of giving clear and convincing arguments for them. If I can bring this off, I should hope and expect that it would have an important bearing, directly or indirectly, on how a man should live his life and how we should order society. I remain ambivalent about this, the fox in me warns me how difficult it is and how pretentious it is. Yet it seems to me a task that people should, though with fear and trembling, address themselves to.

But enough of such program constructing, enough of such grandiose talk. Let me tie what I am trying to say to an example by saying something of religion. I shall also illustrate, by way of examples, (1) what I mean by holding philosophical theses, for which I am prepared to give arguments, and (2) to illustrate how these theses, if sound, would be of considerable importance for our lives. It has long been a conviction of mine—a conviction that has survived several changes in philosophical orientation—that there is no reason, no intellectual justification or moral need to believe in God. I am convinced that religious beliefs should belong to the tribal folklore of mankind and there is no more need to believe in God than there is to believe in Santa Claus or the Easter Bunny. We do not need such beliefs to give our lives meaning or to undergird the moral life, and such beliefs are not essential for an understanding of the nature and destiny of man. The great religions do indeed contain bits which can serve as aspirational ideals, but in this respect there is nothing there that is not perfectly available to the atheist. That is to say, for *some* people religion may be of value as a kind of "moral poetry," but even in this way, it is not something essential to the human animal. Some people can get on very well without it. Man, I believe, should prize truth and should try to live according to what Freud called "the reality principle." But if he is to do this, he must reject the claims of religion. Here is my commitment. Let us have a look at how I can support it.

Let me state this conviction a little more fully and a little more exactly in the form of three philosophical theses. I shall then defend them and illustrate how I use philosophical analysis in their defense.

1. The ultimate basis or rationale of our morality cannot be grounded in our belief in God or in our belief that ultimate reality is being itself (whatever that may mean) or in anything of that order. In fact, just the reverse is the case, only if we already have some moral understanding, some *knowledge* of good and evil, could we ever come to believe that there is a God or properly understand what people are talking about when they speak of God.

2. When religious people talk of the love, mercy, and the omnipotence of God or even of His reality, they make statements which are either patently false, most probably false, or are, in a significant sense, unintelligible. Furthermore, modern theologians such as Buber, Tillich, Robinson, and Bultmann are no improvement on the traditional supernaturalists, for they either say, in extravagant Hegeloid jargon, something that is identical with what an atheist would or could consistently say or they engage in a kind of obscurantist gobbledygook that is as unintelligible as anything traditional supernaturalists tried to say. "There is a God" like "There is a Santa Claus" is a bit of mythology for it is

either patently false, grossly improbable, or without the significant factual content it purports to have.

3. The claim, so characteristic of modern apologetics, that atheists are really believers in disguise, is not correct. Furthermore, there need be nothing either shallow, confused, or backwoodsy about atheism, and atheism is not itself, as such apologists claim, another religion. It is not even an *Ersatz*-religion.

Let us, in examining my first thesis, have a look at a fairly orthodox characterization of God. I take it from Pope Pius XI's Encyclical *Mit brennender Sorge*. In 1937, addressing himself to German Catholics, Pius XI first tells us what God is not:

> Take care, Venerable Brethren, that above all, faith in God, the first and irreplaceable foundation of all religion, be preserved in Germany pure and unstained. The believer in God is not he who utters the name in his speech, but he for whom this sacred word stands for a true and worthy concept of the Divinity. Whoever identifies, by pantheistic confusion, God and the universe, by either lowering God to the dimensions of the world, or raising the world to the dimensions of God, is not a believer in God. Whoever follows that so-called pre-Christian Germanic conception of substituting a dark and impersonal destiny for the personal God, denies thereby the Wisdom and Providence of God. . . .
>
> Whoever exalts race, or the people, or the State, or a particular form of State, or the depositories of power, or any other fundamental value of the human community—however necessary and honorable be their function in wordly things—whoever raises these notions above their standard value and divinizes them to an idolatrous level, distorts and perverts an order of the world planned and created by God: he is far from the true faith in God and from the concept of life which that faith upholds.[3]

Then Pius goes to to tell us what God really is. "Our God is the Personal God, supernatural, omnipotent, infinitely perfect, one in the Trinity of Persons, tri-personal in the unity of divine essence, the Creator of all existence, Lord, King and ultimate Consummator of the history of the world, who will not, and cannot, tolerate a rival god by His side." Orthodox Christians—Catholics and Protestants alike—have, until recently at least, all been asked to believe in such a God; and if we delete the part about the trinity of persons, we have a concept of Deity that is also integral to Judaism and Islam. There is much more to these religions than the asserting of certain dogmas, but one thing integral to these religions is just such a belief in God. It is presupposed in all the rest that a Christian and Jew does; it is presupposed in the rest of their religious activities. The core notion of such a Deity can be briefly put as follows: "God is the sole, supernatural, omnipotent, infinitely perfect creator and director of all finite existence." Now, in order to examine my first thesis, let us assume—what surely is to assume a lot—that such a statement is perfectly intelligible and a tolerably adequate characterization of God and let us also assume that there in fact is such a reality. In order to appraise my first thesis, let us now consider the relations between this God and morality. For a bit let us neglect, in asking this question, the phrase "infinitely perfect" in this characterization of God. Just consider (1) "There is a single, supernatural, omnipotent creator and director of all finite existence." What follows from this about what we *ought* to do and what would be good to do and what things, actions or attitudes, if any, are of *ultimate value*? The answer is nothing: (1) purports to be a factual statement and from a purely factual statement or from a set of factual statements no normative conclusions can be deduced. One cannot get a normative statement, directive of human behavior and/or attitudes, from purely non-normative statements.

To this it may be replied that while we cannot derive an *ought* from an *is*, we can and do all the time use factual statements to support our normative judgments. This is indeed true. Furthermore the existence of a single, supernatural, omnipotent creator and director of all finite existence would be a fact of great relevance to a believer. Given that fact (assuming now that it is a fact) and given the further fact that this Being commands a certain thing, a believer would most certainly judge that he ought to do what this being commands. But why, we might very well ask? His being creator of man and all finite existence, his being the omnipotent director of all finite existence does not *prove* or in any way establish his goodness, does not show that He is *worthy* of being obeyed. He might, with those attributes, even be a malevolent deity. After all, what did Job learn when God spoke to him out of the whirlwind but that God was marvelously powerful, that God was his creator and the like? Given God's behavior to Job and given God's pact with Satan, it would have been more reasonable for Job to have concluded with Schopenhauer that God is evil. How does power, intelligence, and creativity by itself show goodness?

If the Christians' picture of the world is true, we ultimately owe our existence to God and, given that we *prize* our existence, we should be glad of that. But this surely does not exhibit His goodness any more than the fact that we proximately owe our existence to the hot night of our father's desire exhibits our father's goodness. Given God's power and intelligence, it is certainly prudent to follow the commandments and directives of God. No one wants to suffer. But, in the heyday of their power, it would also have been prudent to follow the directives of a Hitler or a Stalin if you were under their hegemony. But these are prudential reasons for acting in one way rather than another. We have not yet found any *moral* reason for doing as God commands.

Well, we should do what God commands for God is all wise and perfectly good. It is only by dropping part of the Pope's characterization of God that we made difficulties for ourselves here. The Pope, as all believers do, conceives of God as being infinitely perfect.

Granting this conception, as surely we must, let us now ask: how do they or how can we come to *know* that God is infinitely perfect. Granted that a believer assumes it or presupposes it, why does he? What reasons does he have for his presupposition? And how could the man without faith come to know that God is infinitely perfect or even good?

Suppose we say: "Here is where we need Revelation, the Bible and an awareness of the concrete actions of God. Here is where our knowledge of Jesus is essential. Jesus the mediator through his moral perfection teaches us something of the infinite perfection of God. We see in gentle Jesus wisdom and goodness and thus we come to know the little we can know of the infinite goodness of God."

Now one might dispute about Jesus' perfection: one might wonder why *this* Bible, *this* putative revelation rather than that? Why the Bible rather than the *Koran* or the *Upanishads*, the *Kalevala*, the *Bhagavadgita* or the *Lotus of the Good Law*?

But all such questions aside, let us for the sake of the argument assume that Jesus is perfect and The Old and New Testaments are the sole ultimate source of genuine revelation, still it is we finite creatures who saw in Jesus' behavior perfection and goodness. Using our own finite moral powers, we recognized that Jesus was this moral exemplar pointing to the infinite perfection of God; beyond that we also recognized that the parables of the Bible were so *noble* and *inspiring* that the Bible *ought* to be taken as our model in moral matters. But these things show, as clearly as can be, that in making these moral assessments we already have a moral criterion, quite independent of the Bible, God, and Jesus, in virtue of which we make these moral judgments.

The believer should say, I think, if he has his wits about him, that he doesn't have and can't have *reasons* for his assertion, anymore than I can have reasons for my assertion that all bachelors are males for, "God is infinitely perfect" is true by definition. It is, in the language of modern philosophy, analytic and this is why it is not open for the believer to question the goodness or perfection of God. Nothing within Christian and Jewish discourse would be called "God" unless it were also called "all good" and "infinitely perfect." This requirement is built into the very logic of God-talk and thus there can be no justification of it or no question of giving evidence for it. Believer and non-believer alike must recognize that within such religious discourse "God is *not* infinitely perfect" is a contradiction.

But doesn't this show, as clearly as anything could, that my first thesis is unsound? Not in the slightest. I can most economically show this in the following way: "God" in such discourses functions as a proper name, though indeed, like "Churchill" and "Mussolini" and unlike your names and mine, a name that takes certain fixed descriptions. Now as a proper name it must make reference, it must denote, it must stand for something that at least conceivably could exist. Now when we say something is good or bad, perfect or imperfect, we are not simply applying a certain descriptive predicate to it. We are not just characterizing it as having a certain property that could, directly or indirectly, be discovered by observation. What we are doing when we ascribe value to something is very difficult to say; sometimes we are expressing our approval of it, taking some interest in it, commending it and the like, but one thing is clear: "good" or "per-

fect" are not property words like "red" or "hard." We could
not discover some action or person to be good by simply observing it quite independently of any attitudes we might take toward
it. Now in considering the concept of God think for a moment
only of what the term "God" purports to refer to. From what we
observe in the world what could be given in an encounter with
God or what could be postulated as actual characteristics of the
deity? That is, we note our finitude and dependency and this
leads us to conceive of a non-dependent, infinite being. Considering only this—considering that infinite but unique non-
spatio-temporal individual that is supposed to be the *denotatum*
of our word "God"—how do you know, from simply in some
way being aware of the reality of that entity, that this individual
is good or infinitely perfect? How can you know, except through
your own limited, finite, fallible moral judgments concerning
any X whatsoever that it is infinitely perfect or for that matter
even perfect or good, where X is simply a force, creator, first
cause, ground of being, whether spatio-temporal or non-spatio-
temporal, finite or infinite? The answer is that you can't and thus
in the most fundamental respect your moral judgments can't
be derived from or based upon the fact that there is or is not a
reality, some force or supernatural being or ground of being,
whom some people call "God." "X is a powerful creator of
everything other than himself, a director and sustainer of the
universe but all the same X is evil" is perfectly possible. That
such a Being *says* he is good, *says* he is infinitely perfect does not
prove that he is, even if he is omniscient and omnipotent. How
can we know or have reason to believe, except by making up our
own minds that he or it is perfect or good? Fallible though our
insight is, we must rely on it here.

When we decide to use the label "God" for this alleged Power
or, if you will, this ground of being, we imply that this reality is
infinitely perfect, but we are able to do this only because we have
a prior and logically independent moral understanding that could
not have been derived simply from discovering that there is a
reality transcendent to the world, a reality that created man and
sustains him, or from discovering that there is some being *as
such*, some ground of being, that is the dimension of depth in the
natural. In this crucial way morality, even Christian morality,
must be independent of religion. In fact just the reverse is the

case, for before we can intelligibly decide that some reality is worthy of worship and thus properly called "God" or some reality is ultimately gracious, to use the obscure talk of Macquarrie and Robinson, and thus our God, we must have some independently arrived at concept of worthiness or graciousness. Thus in a very crucial sense religion presupposes a moral understanding that is logically independent of religion and not, as Brunner, Kierkegaard, and Barth would have it, just the reverse. To say this is not an expression of human hubris, but simply a matter of logic.

Someone might very well accept this *logical* point and still insist that I miss an important *psychological* point about how religions reinforce the moral beliefs of many people. I recall a psychiatrist once saying to me, after I had given a lecture on psychoanalysis and religion, that while he didn't need religion, while many people didn't need religion, a significant number of people who came to him for help very much needed their religion to attain psychological stability. Their chance of finding any significance in their lives, and no doubt their ability to hold onto any effective moral orientation, was tied for all practical purposes to their holding onto their religious beliefs. But he also agreed that if they had been differently indoctrinated, soberly educated without these religious myths, they would not need this religious crutch. Yet his central point was that if we look at the actual, concrete situation, it is manifest that many people need their religion to give meaning to their lives. Many men know what they should do, but can't bring themselves to do it, many need the moral imagery, the parables, the stories of their religions; and they very much need the solidarity, the sense of belonging, that religion gives them. Without their religion they would as a matter of fact lose their aspirational ideals; their capacity for moral endeavour would be blighted. In a word, they need religion to put their heart into virtue.

Nothing I have said was calculated to deny this or even underplay it, though I should not like to see it apologetically overplayed into the Pascalian theme that *all* men need religion to give significance and moral orientation to their lives. But a recognition of this psychological truth does nothing to show how our knowledge of good and evil does or even can rest on our belief in God or in our knowledge that such a reality exists. It only shows how some men with an understanding of good and evil need a *prod* and *crutch* to continue to act as moral agents.

No doubt most people, in point of origin, get their moral beliefs from their religions in the sense that moral talk for many is first introduced in the context of religious talk, and later, psychologically speaking, they need to associate difficult moral endeavours with these religious pictures. But questions of *validity* are independent of *origin*. Such a psychological account says nothing whatsoever about how we can justify moral beliefs or about our *knowledge* of good and evil. This, as I have shown, is independent of religion. Furthermore, it does not show that all people need such images or that moral belief and significant moral endeavour could not survive and would not have a point in the twilight or even in the complete absence of the gods.

I shall now support my second thesis. Religion, as Hepburn has wisely reminded us, should not be identified with its doctrinal formulae; furthermore the great religions of the world have a unity, amidst a very considerable internal complexity, that makes it difficult to understand their central doctrinal claims in isolation.[4] Yet in stressing this, one must not make a new "myth of the whole," one must not neglect the fact that presupposed in these religions are certain very mysterious allegedly factual claims. And if they are truly factual claims, as they appear to be, they must have a certain logical character. For any statement p to be a bona fide factual statement the assertion and denial of p must *not* be equally compatible with any conceivable observation that might be made. If p and not-p have exactly the same empirical consequences, if everything that is logically possible for us to experience is equally compatible with the truth and falsity, or the probable truth and falsity, of p and not-p then p and not-p are *not* factual statements, whatever p and not-p may be. This, of course, does not mean that in every respect they are meaningless. (In fact the ability to deny p implies that in *some sense p* is intelligible.) But what I have said above does show that p and not-p are devoid of factual significance or intelligibility if such conditions obtain. In short they could not be statements of fact.

Religious people, however, do believe that certain of their very central religious doctrines are statements of fact. They presuppose "there is a God"—that they do not utter it very often is logically irrelevant—and they believe "God created the world." Both of these statements they take to be factual statements.

A sufficiently anthropomorphic believer—someone who thinks that in *some way* it is literally possible to see God—might well use these statement as bona fide factual statements. For him God would be very much like the Homeric gods except that his monotheism commits him to taking God to be a loner and not the head of a clan of gods. But it is simply superstitious to believe in *such* a god. What evidence do we have for such a god up there or out there?[5] Who has observed him under controlled conditions? Why is it that the Eskimos see Sedena, a female God, who lives in the sea and not on the land and who controls the storms, the weather, and the sea mammals, while the Israelites with a very different family structure and very different problems see Yahweh, a God of the desert and a ferocious male God who protects the Israelites from alien peoples? The Alaskan Eskimos by contrast have their risks in the winter sea mammal hunting; here they meet some of the crucial crises of their lives. The anthropomorphic deities of the various cultures are tailor-made projectively to meet the anxieties and emotional needs of their members.[6] It isn't a question of first seeing or somehow apprehending Sedena or Yahweh and then making certain claims. It is rather a matter of projecting certain needs onto the universe and then making up stories about these deifications. Our divinities are fashioned projectively to fit our cultural preoccupations.

Even more fundamentally—all questions of origin apart—who has seen or in any way apprehended Sedena, Yahweh, Zeus, Wotan or Fricka? We have no good evidence for their existence. Belief in such anthropomorphic deities is intelligible enough. "Fricka exists" or "there is a God" are in such a context something we can understand. But to believe that there are such anthropomorphic divinities is just a bald superstition. To believe that there are such gods is like believing that there is a Santa Claus or that there are fairies.

But sophisticated believers and, I believe, even most plain believers for a long time have ceased believing in such anthropomorphic gods. God is neither up there, down there or out there in any literal sense. God is not a reality you can see or even apprehend. God is thought to be transcendent to the whole cosmos, the creator and sustainer of this cosmos, but He is still somehow a person, an individual—though an infinite individual—who is non-identifiable, non-spatio-temporal, and in no spatio-temporal relation with the world.[7] The object of our discourse when we discourse of God—when we talk *to* as well as *about* God—is taken to be an infinite, non-spatio-temporal particular named by the name "God." But given this sophisticated use, "There is a God" or "God created the world" are not false but unfalsifiable statements, completely incapable of being confirmed or disconfirmed. No matter how much order we see in the world, the non-believer can deny what the believer affirms with as much and with as little plausibility. He can quite consistently, after taking note of this order, assert that there is no God and that the observed order is just a natural part of the world; likewise no matter how much evil and disorder there is, the believer can speak of man's corruption and God's inscrutable grace. The believer can and does go on making his affirmations, no matter what happens and the non-believer can and does make his denials no matter what happens. Try this little experiment for yourselves: if you think of yourselves as believers, what *conceivable* turn of observable events would make you say you were mistaken or probably mistaken in holding that belief; and if you think of yourself as an atheist or as an agnostic try this experiment on yourself: what *conceivable* turn of observable events, if only you were to observe them, would make you say you were mistaken or probably mistaken in denying or doubting that it is true or probably true that there is a God? If the God you believe in, deny, or doubt, is anything like the non-anthropomorphic God I have just characterized, I predict you will not be able to answer that question. But if this is so, and I think it is, then your alleged God-statements "there is a God" "or "God created the world" are devoid of *factual* significance. They are then equally compatible with anything and everything that the believer and non-believer alike can conceive as being experienceable. This being the case, they are no more saying anything that is in reality incompatible, than the American is asserting anything that the Englishman is not when the American calls all those things and only those things elevators that the Englishman calls lifts. The man, in such a circumstance, who says "there is a God" is not asserting anything incompatible with or even different from the statement of a man who says "there is no God." But this shows that neither statement has factual content; neither succeeds in asserting nor denying the existence of the peculiar reality that they were meant to assert or deny. Belief, paradoxically enough, becomes indistinguishable from atheism. But this, in effect, shows that such a believer has not succeeded in showing how he can make a claim to reveal a reality or reveal some level of reality that the non-believer does not grasp. The realm of the supernatural remains unrecognizable.

We are no better off, if like Tillich and Robinson, we reject supernaturalism and claim that to speak of God being transcendent to the cosmos is to speak metaphorically or that to speak of the creation of the world by God is to speak metaphorically, for we are still saddled with very similar difficulties. Consider the following sentences, sentences that are used to make central claims within their theologies.

1. There is being itself.
2. There is a creative ground of being and meaning.
3. The *agape* of the cross is the last word about Reality.
4. Reality is not ultimately impersonal or neutral; it is ultimately gracious.
5. God is the beyond in the midst of our lives.

Apply the same tests to these statements. What conceivable experiences would lend probability to any of these statements, would make it more or less reasonable to believe them to be true? What would confirm or disconfirm them where they are taken to affirm something incompatible with what a non-believer could say? These obscurantist statements are no more capable of supporting belief than are the familiar claims of traditional theism. You are being deluded if you think people like Tillich, Bultmann or Robinson will take you beyond the chains of illusion. All you are doing is substituting an unfamiliar absurdity for a familiar one.

There is an important objection to my arguments that deserves careful attention. Such an objector agrees "there is a God," is intended, when believers use it in typical contexts, to assert a fact.[8] He would stress, as I would, that it most certainly is not intended simply to express a person's attitude toward the world or simply to guide conduct or alter behaviour. But, he would add, we must not forget there are all kinds of assertions and many kinds of factual statements. By taking "there is a God" to be a contingent factual statement asserting a contingent fact or a "contingent state-of-affairs" one distorts the actual logic of God-talk. We must not violate the integrity of God-talk by forcing upon it alien rules or alien criteria. If we, as we should, consider how "God" and "there is a God" are actually used in religious contexts, we will come to see that the existence of God cannot be taken to be a "contingent fact," and if "there is a God" cannot be taken to be "a contingent fact" then the proposition which asserts the existence of God cannot, it is argued, be a contingent proposition. "There is a God" must be taken to be logically or necessarily true.

This being so, it, of course, makes no sense to ask how "there is a God" can be verified or falsified, confirmed or disconfirmed, for it is a mark of a logical or necessary truth that it is true a priori. The man who asks for some contingent, empirical state of affairs to verify an a priori or logical statement merely shows that he does not understand the statement in question.[9] He shows by his very request, that he doesn't understand what an a priori statement is. Given that "there is a God" is logically and thus necessarily true and that God, the superlatively good and only adequate object of worship, necessarily exists, my request for confirmation or disconfirmation is utterly inappropriate.

But why say God's existence is necessary and that "there is a God" is a logical truth or necessarily true? A crucial and typical employment of "there is a God" is to assert that there is a being, superlatively worthy of worship, who is the sole adequate object of the religious attitude of worship. But an adequate object of such an attitude could not be a being who just happens to exist, or might come to exist or cease to exist or upon whom other beings just happen to depend.[10] Such an object of worship, that is God, must be a being whose nonexistence is wholly unthinkable in any circumstance. There must be no conceivable alternative to such a reality. Since, by definition, God is said to be that reality upon which all other things depend for their very existence, we could not, of course, state even a conceivable state of affairs that would be incompatible with His existence for, for any X if some conceivable state of affairs Y is incompatible with the existence of X, then X by definition could not be God, for Y would attest to the fact that there was something whose existence did not depend on X. Similarly since God's nonexistence is unthinkable under any circumstance (including any conceivable circumstance), God's existence is necessary and "there is a God" is logically true and asserts a "logical fact."

There are a host of objections that can and have been made to arguments of this sort, but I shall here, so as to not go too far afield, limit myself to one.[11] The crucial point I want to make here is just this: in asserting that in calling something "God" we must also say about that object of our discourse that its existence is necessary, its nonexistence wholly unthinkable, it is not at all necessary to construe "necessary" or "the necessity" here as "logically necessary" or "logical necessity."[12] The modal term "necessary" has many uses. As Anscombe and Geach point out "since what is 'necessary' is what 'cannot' not be, to say that 'necessary' can only refer to logical necessity is equivalent to saying that whatever cannot be so, logically cannot be so—e.g., that since I cannot speak Russian, my speaking Russian is logically impossible: which is absurd."[13]

It is true that if something is appropriately designated by the word "God," it cannot not-exist. But it doesn't at all follow from this, what is prima facie implausible, that "there is no God" is a contradiction and "there is a God" is a logical truth. This would only follow if the "cannot" in "cannot not-exist" were a logical cannot, but what evidence do we have that this is so? Surely it looks as if we could significantly deny that there is a God.

That God couldn't just happen to exist, come to exist, cease to exist, if He exists at all, establishes that we conceive of God as an eternal being, but that "God is eternal" is analytic does not at all prove that an eternal being exists or that there are eternal beings. God couldn't come to exist or cease to exist, but it might be the case that there is no God.

That "God" is so defined that other beings are said to be completely dependent on God and that this dependence is not merely fortuitous does not prove that "there is a God" is logically necessary. "There is no completely independent being upon whom all beings depend" or "there is a reality whose existence is necessary for all other beings" can be significantly denied.

God's existence is thought to be necessary; but there is no

good reason at all for thinking His existence is *logically* necessary or "there is a God" is logically true; and there is prima facie,
though perhaps not decisive evidence, for asserting that God's
existence is not logically necessary, namely that existential statements do not appear to be logical truths and that more specifically, "there is no God" does not at all appear to be self-
contradictory or in any way contradictory. When believers say,
as many of them do, that God's nonexistence is wholly unthinkable in any circumstance, they need not be taken to be holding a
theory about the logical status of "there is a God," namely that
it is self-contradictory to deny that God exists. They can be
taken to be asserting that the presence of God is so evident to
them that, given their conception of Him as an eternal being,
they could not, as a matter of psychological fact, in any way find
it thinkable that God should not exist. God's actuality is so
vividly present to believers that they could no more, except in
a purely logical sense, come to doubt for one moment the reality
of God than I could doubt that the earth has existed for many
years and that I have been on or near to the surface of that earth
during my life. I recognize that I can significantly deny these
propositions (after all they are not analytic) but, like Moore, I
am quite certain of them and I find it quite unthinkable that they
might be false. When certain believers tell us that the non-
existence of God (that reality given to them through faith) is
quite unthinkable, it is very plausible to take him to be making
such an assertion.

God's existence is thought to be necessary; that is, if God
exists the existence of God is without beginning or end and without dependence for existence upon any reality other than himself.
But this necessity is not a logical necessity but the *aseity* of the
scholastics or what Hick calls a factual necessity.[14]

Thus it will not do to try to evade my contention that, given
a non-anthropomorphic conception of God, "there is a God," is
not an intelligible factual statement by claiming "there is a God"
is logically true and asserts a "logical fact." There is no con-
vention in English or logical rule which makes "there is no God"
a contradiction. One might, by suitable stipulations and a little
ingenuity, set up an artificial "ideal language" in which, given
certain stipulative meaning-postulates, "there is no God," when
interpreted by that "language," would be a contradiction, but

this would only prove that certain people with certain needs and a certain amount of logical ingenuity had constructed such an artificial language. It would show nothing at all about whether "there is no God," which after all is part of the corpus of English, or its German, Spanish, or Swahili equivalents, is used to make a contradictory statement. In short, it would be of absolutely no avail in showing that the statement that there is no God is a contradiction and its denial a logical truth. Thus there are good grounds for thinking that "there is a God" is *not* a logical truth and there are no good grounds for thinking that it is; but, as even Clarke (a defender of the above view) insists, "there is a God" is surely taken to assert something and it is a statement around which ultimately all theistic discourse revolves.[15] It is not a logical statement asserting a "logical fact"; it is rather intended by believers as a factual statement asserting what, logically speaking, is a "contingent fact." But then our initial questions about confirmation and disconfirmation are perfectly relevant and this criticism of my argument fails. Consider the following: (1) there is a God; (2) there is an eternal being; (3) there is an infinite, non-spatio-temporal individual who never began to exist and never shall *cease* to exist and upon whom all other beings depend. When (1) and (2) are asserted by non-anthropomorphic believers and when (3) is asserted, their asserters do not know what, even in principle, would confirm or disconfirm these putatively factual assertions. Since this is so they are bogus, pseudo-factual statements, devoid of the kind of intelligibility that believers rightly demand of them.

Once we leave a simple but false or highly improbable anthropomorphic theism, we find that the key claims of non-anthropomorphic, truly transcendent theistic beliefs are thought by those who accept these beliefs to be beliefs which are expressed in mysterious yet genuinely factual, non-analytic statements; but these key theological statements, unfortunately, are not factual claims for, being unverifiable in principle, they are devoid of factual significance. In short, key doctrines of Judaism, Christianity, and Islam, doctrines without which these religions would be radically transformed and thoroughly undermined, are confused beliefs, parading as factual beliefs but actually functioning as bits of ideology that distort our understanding of the world and give a delusory support to certain peoples' basic commitments by making them appear to be based on facts, written so to say in the stars.[16] If what I have said in this essay is generally correct one ought to be an atheist and reject religious belief, anthropomorphic or non-anthropomorphic, as irrational and unnecessary.

This brings me to my third and final thesis, namely my thesis about atheism. Kierkegaard and Tillich and many like them claim atheism is impossible. Atheism, in their view, is something like a contradiction for, in their very seriousness, in their very concern to destroy idols, atheists exhibit their belief, i.e., exhibit that in a profound sense they are *not* atheists. There is, as I shall show, an inordinate amount of confusion in such a claim. Atheism is not a kind of religion: it is not incoherent or contradictory; it is a reasonable belief that we all ought to adopt.

But before I go into that there are some important terminological distinctions that ought to be made. The first I owe to my colleague Paul Edwards and the second to the British philosopher Alasdair MacIntyre. Edwards points out that there are two ways in which the word "atheism" is used. Sometimes when a man maintains that there is no God he *simply* means that "there is a God" or "God exists" is false. This rather traditional atheism, as Ayer noted long ago, runs into the difficulty that the putative statement "there is a God" is factually meaningless when "God" is used in its straightforward religious ways. Since this is so there is an important respect in which such putative factual statements are unintelligible. But if "there is a God" is so unintelligible the parallel statement "there is no God" is likewise unintelligible. It does not express a false factual statement. Such an atheism is as nonsensical as such a theism! But, Edwards reminds us, there is a second way in which "atheism" is used, and this use of "atheism" is not entangled in these difficulties: ". . . a person is an atheist if he *rejects* belief in God, regardless of whether his rejection is based on the view that belief in God is false."[17] I think of myself as an atheist in this broader sense. To put the matter more precisely, "God exists" seems to me, depending on how "God" is used, either absurdly false, of such a low order of probability that belief in such a being is superstitious or, in its more characteristic uses, it is devoid of factual content and is thus in a significant sense unintelligible and unworthy of belief. To reject the concept of God for any of these reasons is to be, in this second broader sense, an atheist.

Yet even, acknowledging this important distinction, there are atheists and atheists. As MacIntyre points out, atheism of any of the above types tends to be what he calls a speculative atheism; that is to say its interests are theoretical: it is concerned with pointing out the fallacies in arguments for the existence of God, the unintelligibility of God-talk and the like. Its patron saints are Hume, Russell, and Ayer. But there is another kind of practical-activist atheism, an atheism that *presupposes* the truth of some form of speculative atheism, but goes far beyond it. We indeed must, such atheists argue, remove the mask of supernaturalist error, but, as Nietzsche and Feuerbach stressed, we must also transform man. We must develop the vision and the intelligence to live in a world without God; we must come to understand in some concrete detail how to give significance to our lives in such a world.

We need to see more clearly than most speculative atheists have that it is not argument or speculative wonder that stokes religion in the first place; rather it is emotional need that fathers religious belief. "Religion," as MacIntyre puts it, "is misunderstood if it is construed simply as a set of intellectual errors; it is rather the case that in a profoundly misleading form deep insights, hopes, and fears are being expressed."[18] We must cure man of his need for religion, and not just show the intellectual absurdity of it. We must, as Feuerbach and Marx stressed, transform society so that men will no longer need to turn to religious forms to give inspiration to their lives. We must show how men's visions and aspirations can be de-mythologized, can be embodied in purely secular *social forms*. We must, as Feuerbach, the greatest of all these activist atheists, puts it, change "the friends of God into friends of man, believers into thinkers, worshippers into workers, candidates for the other world into students of this world, Christians, who on their own confession are half-animal and half-angel, into new men—whole men." The patron saints of this kind of atheism are Feuerbach, Marx, Nietzsche, David Strauss, and Freud.

I count myself as such an atheist too—though certainly not as a patron saint. I hope in defending and advocating atheism, without personally engaging in any ideology or propagandistic moves, to establish the theoretical untenability of theistic beliefs, to show we do not need them to justify our moral convictions or to give significance to our lives, and to show that there are other ways of life, other ways of thinking and acting, that are more desirable, more admirable, more *worthy* of allegiance than our religious ways of life. In carrying out this last task, a philosopher must indeed do a little normative ethics and he must dirty his hands with a few empirical facts, but I see no reason why he should not do these things, if only he does not confuse normative ethics with meta-ethics.[19] In this essay I have tried to do something toward establishing the first two points. To establish the third point, one must go into the nasty *detail* of normative argument and into an examination, in some concreteness and with some honesty, of the messy details and harassments of living.

Now I am in a position to examine the rather frequent charge that such atheism, and sometimes indeed all atheism, is not a denial of religion, but in effect and in reality its affirmation, an *Ersatz*-religion of its own.

Will Herberg, reasoning much as Kierkegaard, Tillich, Bultmann, and Bishop Robinson do about these matters, stresses the fact that we should see the "problem of God" not as a speculative affair but as an existential concern. Viewed in that way, he argues there are "on the existential level . . . no atheists."[20] Why not? Because, according to Herberg, "the structure of a human being is such that man cannot live his life, or understand himself, without some ultimate concern that he takes as the that-beyond-which-there-is-nothing of this world. That is indeed his god, and the articulation of his life in terms of it his religion. . . . In this sense every man, by virtue of being human, is *homo religiosus*; every man has his religion and his god. On the existential level, then, the question is not god or no god, religion or no religion; but rather: what *kind* of god? What *kind* of religion?"[21] Luther remarks that "whatever your heart clings to and confides in, that is your god." And Robinson and Tillich tell us that belief in God is a matter of what you take seriously without any reservation. That which ultimately concerns us, that which we finally place our trust in, that is our God. But since every man, and the atheist most fervently, places his trust in something, has some intimate and ultimate concern, no man is *existentially* an atheist or, if you would rather talk that way, atheism is a religion or at the very least an *Ersatz*-religion. "The atheism," Herberg argues, "of a Feuerbach or a young Marx was existentially not atheism at all, but the deification of Man; just as the 'atheism' of the later Marx, and so many Marxists, was actually a quasi-Hegelian deification of the Dialectic of History."[22]

There is a whole evening's worth of confusion in these Kierke-gaardian-Tillichian arguments. I shall only have time to expose a few of them, but that will be quite enough.

1. How do we know, or do we know, that all men or even most men have these *ultimate* concerns? It is truistic that human beings care about things, if only booze, the opposite sex, and getting a new sports car. But does such a concern count as an ultimate concern? Well if it does we are well on our way to making "All men have ultimate concern" stipulatively, but arbitrarily, analytic. If we do not play with words in this way, we certainly need a little raw empiricism, a little sociological and anthropological evidence, that all men have such ultimate concerns and thus man is *homo religiosus*. But these religious apologists do not give us such evidence.[23]

2. Let us, however, suppose we have such evidence. Let us suppose that all men everywhere have their ultimate concerns, have something they are deeply devoted to, committed to and finally put their trust in, it still does not follow at all that all such men are religious, that all such men believe in God, have a god, some sense of a *numinous* reality, or a sense of the divine or anything of that sort. We should beware of essentialist definitions of "religion."[24] Theravada Buddhism, a religion of spiritual liberation, has no God or object of worship and devotion.[25] To achieve nirvana (literally the "going out" as of a flame) is to finally achieve liberation (*moksa*) from the endless series of rebirths of a life that is full of suffering. But the goal of this religion is also a spiritual one; nirvana is a very different concept than God, but like the concept of God it is a transcendental concept, e.g., the Buddhist faithful will not allow that naturalistic accounts of it can be fully adequate. In this way, all religions, besides being matters of ultimate concern, have some concept of the sacred or some concept of spiritual reality. But the atheist repudiates nirvana as fully as God; he rejects thinking in terms of sacred, divine, or spiritual realities. If like Nietzsche, Feuerbach, and

Freud, he is what I have called an activist atheist, he too has his commitments, has his vision of what a good world would be like, has—if you will—his ultimate concerns. But this does not make him religious, except in the perfectly trivial sense that to be religious about anything is to be deeply involved with it and the like; it does not give him a religion or a god, except in another *metaphorical* sense. To place your trust in something, to be ultimately concerned, to be concerned about the meaning of your existence is at best a *necessary* but most surely not a sufficient condition for being religious or having a religion. To have a religion is to have a distinctive ethical outlook, to accept a certain Weltanschauung, but the converse need not be the case. Ethics is not religion and religion is not simply ethics, or ethics touched with emotion, or associated with parable. A practical activist atheist has a normative view, has a Weltanschauung, but no religion. "A religious way of life" is not a redundancy; "a religious Weltanschauung" is not a pleonasm and "an antireligious or areligious ethic or way of life" is not a contradiction, a logical oddity or a deviation from a linguistic regularity.

Herberg argues that on the existential level there are no atheists for atheism is itself a religious affirmation. He has not shown how this is the case and I have given good reasons for denying that it is the case. But Herberg goes beyond this, for according to him atheism is not only religious, it is an idolatrous religion for it deifies man, the dialectic of history or the state. Herberg again confuses having a certain way of life, having a set of ethical and aspirational ideals, with having a religion. But I think it must be admitted that *some* atheists, not sufficiently emancipated from religious thinking, did stupidly deify man. Comte and Saint-Simon are offenders here, and this most surely is ideological thinking and ought to be resisted most strenuously. But no atheist *must* think this way; no atheist should think this way; and most atheists do not think in this confused way. Commitment yes; ideology and religion no. A commitment to a way-of-life need not be a religious commitment or an ideological commitment.

How this is so can be brought out most economically by contrasting a remark Herberg makes about Christianity with a remark I would make about religion. Herberg remarks that "the fundamental conviction of Christianity is the belief in the insufficiency, nay impotence, of man to straighten out his life or

achieve anything worthwhile through his own powers and re-
sources, without reliance on the God beyond."[26] Now I am perfectly aware that there is corruption in the palace of justice; all
my life I have felt keenly in myself and in others the deeply per-
verse Dostoevskian ambivalences of the human animal. Man is,
in Pascal's magnificent phrase, but a frail reed; however, I would
still reply to Herberg that it is either false or factually meaningless to assert that there is "a God beyond" as the ground of being
and meaning, or as the reality transcendent to the cosmos. Such
beliefs are ideological and mythological, and man, frail though
he be, has no such reality to place his trust in or to rely on. Furthermore, man does have some knowledge of good and evil that
not only is but must be independent of any knowledge of a transcendent reality, being-as-such, or a ground of being. Some men
have straightened out their lives, given meaning to their own existence and helped to give meaning to the lives of others by using
their own puny powers and the help of others similarly situated.
To believe that this is so for some men, to *hope* that it may be so
for others, and to work to bring about social and psychological
conditions under which this will be so for as many as possible is
not to engage in ideology, to *deify* man, or to make for oneself
an idolatrous religion, an *Ersatz*-religion, or for that matter any
religion at all.

Notes

1. These remarks about ideology were occasioned by a reading of
Henry Aiken's perceptive essay "The Revolt Against Ideology," *Com-
mentary* 37, no. 4 (1964): 29–30. For an exact account of the nature of
ideological statements see my "On Speaking of God," *Theoria* 28 (1962):
118–125.

2. These remarks were made by Professor Passmore in a lecture
"What is Philosophy?" given to the New York University Philosophy
Club during the spring semester of 1964.

3. Anne Fremantle, ed., *The Papal Encyclicals* (New York: New
American Library, 1956), p. 25.

4. Ronald Hepburn, "A Critique of Humanist Theology," in *Objections to Humanism*, ed. H. J. Blackham (Philadelphia: Lippincott, 1963),
pp. 52–54.

5. Some of the difficulties, evasions, and obscurities are brought out

in Robinson's somewhat sensational book *Honest to God* and in the subsequent volume *The Honest to God Debate.*

6. Weston LaBarre, "Religions, Rorschachs, and Tranquilizers," *The American Journal of Orthopsychiatry* 29 (1959): 688–698.

7. This is most clearly put by I. M. Crombie in his "The Possibility of Theological Statements," in *Faith and Logic*, ed. Basil Mitchell (London: George Allen and Unwin, Ltd., 1957), pp. 31–83.

8. The views I have in mind are clearly expressed by Bowman L. Clarke in his "Linguistic Analysis and the Philosophy of Religion," *The Monist* 47 (Spring 1963): 365–386; and Charles Hartshorne, *The Logic of Perfection* (LaSalle, Illinois: The Open Court Publishing Co., 1962).

9. J. N. Findlay, "Can God's Existence Be Disproved?" in *New Essays in Philosophical Theology* (New York: The Macmillan Co., 1955), pp. 47–57.

10. Ibid., p. 52.

11. Terence Penelhum's essay "Divine Necessity," *Mind* 69 (1960): 175–186, the essays in response to Malcolm's defense of the ontological argument by Allen, Abelson and Penelhum, *The Philosophical Review* (January 1961): pp. 56–92; Robert C. Coburn's, "Professor Malcolm on God," *Australasian Journal of Philosophy* 41 (1963); John O. Nelson, "Modal Logic and the Ontological Proof for God's Existence," *The Review of Metaphysics* 17 (1963); and Adel Daher, "God and Logical Necessity," *Philosophical Studies* (Dublin, Ireland) 18 (1969) all raise effective arguments against some facets of such a position.

12. This is nicely shown by John Hick, "Necessary Being," *Scottish Journal of Theology* 14 (1961): 355–369 and Alvin Plantinga, "Necessary Being," in *Faith and Philosophy*, ed. Alvin Plantinga (Grand Rapids, Michigan: Wm. B. Eerdmans Co., 1964), pp. 97–108.

13. G. E. M. Anscombe and P. T. Geach, *Three Philosophers: Aristotle, Aquinas and Frege* (Oxford: Oxford University Press, 1961), p. 114.

14. John Hick, p. 365.

15. Bowman Clarke, p. 376.

16. Attention to my remarks about ideological statements will help make the nature of such claims clearer.

17. Paul Edwards, "Some Notes on Anthropomorphic Theology," in *Religious Experience and Truth*, ed. Sidney Hook (New York: N.Y.U. Press, 1961), p. 242. See also my "On Being an Atheist," *The Personalist* (Winter 1970).

18. Alasdair MacIntyre, "God and The Theologians," *Encounter* (September 1965), p. 3.

19. For some of the crucial distinctions here and for some of the ways in which we may do normative ethics see my "Speaking of Morals," *The Centennial Review* 2 (1958): 414–444 and Hans Albert, "Ethik and Metaethik," *Archiv für Philosophie* 2 (1961): 28–63.

20. Will Herberg, "God and The Theologians," *Encounter* (November 1963), p. 57.

21. Ibid., p. 56.

22. Ibid., p. 57.

23. I have said something more about this in my "Is God So Powerful

That He Doesn't Even Have to Exist," in *Religious Experience and Truth*, pp. 270–282.

24. Ninian Smart, "Numen, Nirvana and The Definition of Religion," *Church Quarterly Review* (April-June 1959), pp. 216–225.

25. Ninian Smart, "Buddhism and Religious Belief," *The Humanist* 76, no. 2 (1961): 47–50. See also his *A Dialogue of Religions* (London: 1960).

26. Will Herberg, p. 57.

REASON AND REVELATION: A LINGUISTIC DISTINCTION*

Bowman L. Clarke

The impact which contemporary linguistic philosophy has made on theology in Britain and America can hardly be overestimated. Austin Farrer has summarized what he takes to be the consequences of this impact in this way: "The old method of philosophizing about theology was the endeavor to prove. This meant to prove theological conclusions from non-theological premises. . . . Such a method of proceeding is now out of fashion."[1] In place of the "old method" of philosophizing about theology, Farrer proposes a contemporary position which I shall call linguistic pluralism; that is, the position that "every science, art, or manner of speaking is now supposed to find its own justification in its own use."[2] The results of this position in contemporary discussions of religious language have been twofold: first, religious language, in terms of use, justification, and meaning, is isolated from the language of science and even ordinary descriptive discourse. As a result, the relationship between religious language and other languages of our culture becomes problematic and any talk about rational and revealed doctrines becomes impossible. In the words of Farrer, "in such a philosophical climate the difference of status . . . between the demonstrable and the indemonstrable parts of theology, between 'rational' and 'revealed' doctrines largely disappears."[3] Secondly, this isolation of religious language makes problematic the very nature of theological discourse. Witness the many attempts to treat religious language as emotive language,[4] disguised moral discourse,[5] convictional language,[6] or as something entirely unique. In fact, the answers to the nature of religious language have become legion.

It is the purpose of this paper to question the position of lin-

*This essay appeared in somewhat different form as "The Language of Revealed Theology," *Journal of Bible and Religion* 32 (October 1964): 334–341.

guistic pluralism as a solution to the problem of theological discourse and to propose that theological doctrines are intended to be, whatever other function they might have, descriptive statements—that is, statements describing or asserting something about God. And I shall attempt to show how theological doctrines may be taken as descriptive statements and the traditional distinction between rational and revealed doctrines may be meaningfully preserved. Perhaps this is only another attempt to rush in where angels fear to tread, but I think the attempt is justified for three reasons. First, I think that most attempts to treat theological doctrines as something other than descriptive discourse have, on the whole, failed, for it is quite clear that, at least in the Christian tradition, doctrinal expressions have generally been taken as describing states-of-affairs, not as expressing emotions, or as merely stating an intention to lead a particular way of life. Certainly some religious utterances are intended to be precisely that, but to maintain that all theological doctrines are of this nature, is simply to maintain that people have been using language in a way which they themselves would deny. Secondly, I do not think that modern developments in logic have forced theology to retreat into a position of linguistic isolation in order to salvage some kind of meaning for its language. There are alternative possibilities. Thirdly, such an isolation of the use, justification, and meaning of theological discourse runs the risk of isolating religion itself and its language in such a way that it becomes unrelated, if not irrelevant, to the general intellectual and cultural environment in which it finds itself. The very nature of religion cries out against this isolation.

In attempting to show how theological doctrines may be taken as descriptive statements, I am limiting myself solely to a methodological problem and only to the problem as it arises in the Christian tradition. In other words, I am not the least bit concerned with the truth or falsity of any Christian theological doctrine. This is the theologian's task; the logician's task is solely concerned with methodology, that is, the conditions under which the theological doctrines may be taken as descriptive statements.

Before rushing in where at least contemporary theologians and philosophers fear to tread, let me be clear as to what I mean by reason and revelation, or rational as opposed to revealed doctrines. It is most important to make this distinction between revealed and rational doctrines on the basis of how one is able to justify a particular doctrine, rather than on the basis of how one might have come to accept or to hold a doctrine. It would not be appropriate, for example, for someone to say: "The doctrine of the existence of God is not a rational doctrine because no one comes to believe in the existence of God from thinking about it; they first accept it on faith." It may be quite true that most people do, in fact, first accept the doctrine of the existence of God on faith, simply because their mother or Sunday School teacher told them that it was true, but this is merely a biographical fact about the believer. It has nothing to do with how one might be able to justify the doctrine as true.

Rational doctrines have traditionally been considered as those doctrines concerning God which can be justified by human beings on the basis of a rational methodology, while revealed doctrines were those doctrines concerning God which could not be so justified by human beings and had to be accepted as true on the basis of faith. St. Thomas,[7] for example, readily admits that many accept the doctrine of the existence of God on the basis of faith, but he insists that it is a rational doctrine, rather than a revealed doctrine, since according to him it can be justified by human beings on the basis of a rational methodology. Thus, only those doctrines which cannot be so justified will be taken as revealed doctrines.

By a rational method, I mean no more than the method which we use in making true and false statements about the common world disclosed to us in experience and the techniques which we have for discerning whether or not the truth conditions of these statements hold. And by a statement I mean no more than a descriptive sentence for which conditions can be given under which we would consider the statement true or false. This methodology should be as applicable to the statements which form a theory in physics and the statements of mathematics as it is to the statements which we make in ordinary discourse, such as the statement, "the University of Georgia Chapel is white."

Such a rational method has two aspects: one concerns the structure of the descriptive language used and the other the means and techniques used for verifying or falsifying the statements. The first is a problem for logic, the second a problem of technology, so let us consider these two problems separately. The linguistic structure, or what I shall call the linguistic framework, of a descriptive language is the set of axioms and rules involved in using the linguistic symbols descriptively. One needs, for example, a set of rules of formation for the statements which specify what will be taken as linguistic symbols and how these symbols may be combined properly to form statements. These rules would include a list of primitive, or undefined symbols, which are used as the basis for the definitions in the language, and a list of formation rules which specify what combinations of these symbols will be taken as statements. Also, one needs a set of transformation rules which list the primitive statements, or axioms, and stipulative rules of inference whereby statements may be inferred from other statements. The axioms, or primitive statements, will be those which must be taken as primitive since they cannot be inferred from or proven on the basis of the other statements. These axioms specify the properties which the primitive or undefined symbols will have. The rules of formation and transformation compose the syntactical rules of the descriptive language.

In addition to the syntactical rules one needs a set of rules which we will call rules of designation. These rules stipulate the designata for our linguistic symbols, or specify what it is the symbols stand for. In addition to these rules of designation, we need a set of rules which give us the truth conditions for our statements. This latter group of rules, usually called the semantical rules, give us the interpretation of our descriptive language and answer the question, what do our signs mean; for to know the truth conditions of a statement is to know the meaning of that statement.

Let me illustrate with the statement, "The University of Georgia Chapel is white." If this sentence is taken as a descriptive statement, then our syntactical rules would have to specify that all the symbols appearing in the statement are acceptable linguistic symbols, and that these symbols are combined in an acceptable order. The following string of symbols, "University the Chapel Georgia of is," would, on the other hand, not be a descriptive statement since the symbols are combined improperly. The semantical rules, in contrast, would specify for us the interpretation, or meaning, of the statement. The rules of designation would tell us that the phrase "the University of Georgia

Chapel" is a name designating this particular building, and that the word "white" is a predicate designating a particular visual quality. The rules which give us the truth conditions for the statement would tell us that the statement is true if, and only if, under normal conditions of sunlight and human vision, this building appears white.

The second aspect of a rational methodology, or the problem of verification, is the practical problem of determining whether or not the truth conditions for a statement do in fact hold. In other words, this is the technological problem of finding out the best technique for determining whether or not these conditions do in fact hold. In the case of our statement "the University of Georgia Chapel is white," the best method seems to be for us to go to the chapel during the daylight hours with normal vision and see whether or not the building appears white. If it does the statement is true; if not, it is false.

Let us look now at the problem of primitive or undefined symbols and the axioms which govern them. In any linguistic framework what will be taken as primitive symbols and axioms depends upon what it is that the language is designed to talk about, namely the subject matter. We began by saying that we were concerned with a rational methodology for making true and false statements about the common world disclosed in experience. Our decision, then, as to what will be taken as primitive symbols and axioms depends upon what we mean by the phrase "the common world disclosed in experience." The task of explicating this phrase by determining the necessary primitive terms and axioms seems to constitute the traditional task of metaphysics, at least in the classical sense of the word. It certainly bears a striking resemblance to what Aristotle termed the search for first principles. Obviously, I cannot solve the metaphysical task in this paper, but I would like to suggest the line which, I think, such a solution should take.

It would seem that any linguistic framework adequate to our task would certainly include some generally accepted set of logical axioms and their primitive symbols, such as "$\cdot$," "$\sim$," "(x)." Also we would like to talk about sets of things which compose this common world and to be able to make such statements as "there are two people on this platform." Consequently, we would have to include some formulation of the axioms of set theory, or type theory, with their primitive symbol "ϵ." In short, this is to say that we would need mathematics as a part of our linguistic framework. But granting these two sets of axioms, they do not specify what kinds of things compose this common world disclosed to us in experience. What we need in addition to these axioms is a set of axioms which specify what kind of individuals compose this common world. It would certainly seem that what we mean by the phrase, "the common world disclosed in experience," is a group of individuals related by spatio-temporal extension and qualitative similarity. Certainly we could not mean less than this. There have been preliminary attempts to construct axioms characterizing these relations in what is called the calculus of individuals, but these attempts are still somewhat in their formative stages and have not reached nearly the general acceptance as have the axioms of logic and set theory.

For the purposes of our discussion, however, let us assume that we have as axioms for our linguistic framework the logical axioms, the axioms of set theory, and the axioms for a calculus of individuals, along with their primitive symbols. Now given these axioms and rules, there will be two kinds of statements which we can make with reference to truth conditions. There will be one set of statements whose truth conditions can be determined to hold solely by examining our rules and axioms. For example, we can determine the statement "the University of Georgia Chapel is white or the University of Georgia Chapel is not white," to be true merely by examining our axioms and rules without going to the Chapel in daylight to make any observations. Any person who has ever constructed a truth table can easily see this. Likewise, since we have the axioms of mathematics, we could determine that the statement "$2 + 2 = 4$" is true without making any observations whatever of the things composing our common world. Mathematicians do this quite frequently. All such statements whose truth or falsity can be determined solely on the basis of our axioms and other rules will be called necessary statements. For they will turn out to be true or false, whichever the case may be, no matter what we observe about the things which make up our world. All the other statements, that is those statements whose truth or falsity cannot be determined on the basis of our rules and axioms, will be called contingent statements. Now the only way in which we can determine the truth or falsity of these contingent statements is by examining what I have called the common world and accumulating evidence that the truth conditions do in fact hold, in much the same way as we would verify the statement "the University of Georgia Chapel is white."

If we accept this brief sketch as an outline of a rational methodology, I think we can justifiably say that to accept a statement as true when the truth conditions have been determined to hold or when there is more evidence that they do hold than that they do not is to entertain a rational belief. And to accept a statement as true when the truth conditions have been determined not to hold or that there is more evidence against them than for them, is to entertain an irrational belief. On the other hand, to accept a statement as true when there is no more evidence for its truth than against it, is to entertain a non-rational belief. In other words, this would be a statement which could be meaningfully formulated according to our linguistic rules, that is, the truth conditions could be given for the statement, but it would not be within the power of human beings to determine whether or not the truth conditions do in fact hold. The limitation here is not due to the logical problem of our linguistic framework; rather it is a technological limitation due to our lack of a technique for verification. It is statements of this kind which supposedly compose revealed doctrines according to St. Thomas. They are non-rational beliefs and must be accepted solely on the basis of faith. It is the task of this paper to show how there may be such statements. First, however, let us consider the problem of rational doctrines, and see how, given our rational methodology, they may be treated. As an illustration, let us take the doctrine of the existence of God. Our problem here is not to prove the existence of God, but rather to suggest how it could be handled in the rational methodology outlined here.

The acceptable procedure for attacking this problem, it seems, would be to analyze some of the traditional ontological and cosmological arguments for the existence of God and see what it is that they are all about. First, let us look at what has traditionally been called the ontological argument, particularly St. Anselm's second formulation of the argument, for it avoids the thorny problem of "existence" being used as a predicate. St. Anselm begins his argument by offering a definite description for the term "God"—that is, a characterization belonging to one and only one individual which he calls "God." What he uses as a definite description of God is the phrase, "that than which nothing greater can be conceived." And his argument for the existence of God runs as follows:

> it is possible to conceive of a being which cannot be conceived not to exist. Hence, if that than which nothing greater can be conceived, can be conceived not to exist, it is not that than which nothing greater can be conceived. But this is an irreconcilable contradiction. There is, then, so truly a being than which nothing greater can be conceived to exist, that it cannot even be conceived not to exist.[8]

Let me summarize this argument in four steps and take the liberty of rephrasing it in terms of our proposed rational methodology.

1. It is possible to formulate a definite description of an individual such that the statement asserting its existence is necessarily true.
2. Such an individual is greater than an individual for which the statement asserting its existence is only contingently true.
3. It follows from step two that God, that than which nothing greater can be conceived, cannot be an individual for which the statement asserting its existence is only contingently true.
4. It follows then from step one and step three that God necessarily exists.

Now what has St. Anselm shown in his argument? It is simply that if it is possible to formulate an adequate definite description for God, then the statement asserting his existence must be necessarily true. For if the statement were not necessarily true, then we would simply not be talking about what we mean by the term, "God." In short, what he has shown us is that the problem of the existence of God is no more than the problem of constructing an adequate and consistent definite description for the term "God"—that is, giving a consistent and adequate meaning for the term. In fact, in his reply to Gaunilo, St. Anselm summarizes his argument in almost these very words; he writes: "If such a being can be conceived to exist, necessarily it does exist."[9] But what St. Anselm has failed to show us is that it is possible to conceive of such an individual,[10] or in terms of our methodology, he has not shown us that one can formulate an adequate and consistent definite description for the term "God" such that the statement asserting his existence is necessarily true.

It seems to me, however, that this is precisely the role of the various cosmological arguments for the existence of God. Let us take, as examples, St. Thomas's "Five Ways," or arguments for the existence of God.[11] His five arguments begin with some general characteristics of the sensible world, and in all five cases he attempts to demonstrate that there is involved in these general characteristics the conception of an individual which necessarily exists. In the first argument he takes the general fact of motion, or change; in the second, efficient causality; the third, contingent, or dependent, individuals; the fourth, gradations of value; in the fifth, rational order. Now we are not at all concerned with the validity of these five arguments, nor with the truth or falsity of their premises; we are only concerned with asking the question: what kind of argument is St. Thomas proposing?

Like St. Anselm, St. Thomas proposes various definite descriptions, or characterizations, for God. But in order to assure the meaningfulness of these definite descriptions, he formulates them in terms of the general characteristics which were used to characterize the sensible world. For the general characteristic of motion, or change, he proposes the first mover; for efficient causality, the first efficient cause; for contingency, the non-contingent, or necessary, individual; for gradations of value, the cause of all value; and for rational order, the intelligent cause of all rational order. And his arguments are attempts to demonstrate that these general characteristics logically necessitate the existence of this individual. As Professor Harrison has put it:

> It follows, for Aquinas, that someone is involved in a contradiction if he affirms the statements "there are things which change" and "there are things which come into being and pass away," and at the same time denies the statements "there is a supreme unmoved mover" and "there is an absolutely necessary being."[12]

In no case, then, do the arguments rest upon the existence of any particular individuals in the sensible world, they rest merely upon the fact that there is a sensible world at all. Consequently, the truth or falsity of the statement, "God exists," is for St. Thomas independent of the truth or falsity of any contingent statement whatever. To quote Professor Harrison again, "the proofs do not require the discovery of any new empirical data, which the method of the natural sciences would call for."[13] On the contrary, the statement asserting the existence of God cannot be either verified or falsified on the basis of any observation; it can only be shown to follow from the axioms which we use to characterize the common world disclosed to us in experience. This, of course, should not be a surprise; for after all, one of the main notions involved in the idea of God is that of the creator of the world. Consequently, it should be irrelevant exactly what individuals make up the world—God would still exist as creator. Therefore, no particular individual creature included in what we call the common world could count either for or against the existence of the creator—only the fact that there are creatures at all.

In terms of what we have called a rational methodology, the problem of the existence of God, as a rational problem, turns out to be the problem of constructing an adequate description for the term, "God," in terms of our primitive symbols and demonstrating that the statement asserting his existence is a necessarily true statement—that is, that its truth conditions would hold no matter what particular individuals make up the particular world disclosed to us in experience. An additional problem, however, would be to define the various traditional attributes of God, such as, omnipresence, omniscience, omnipotence, goodness, etc., in terms of our primitive signs and to show that these divine attributes necessarily follow from the definite description and the accepted axioms. Of course it is not our present task to do this; that is the task of the systematic theologian. The logician's task is simply to show how the problem should be treated in a rational methodology. In order that we may turn to the doctrines of revealed theology, however, let us assume that the theologian has succeeded in his task. And if he has succeeded in this task, there will perhaps be certain meaningful statements which can be made about God, but which will be neither necessarily true, nor necessarily false, since we cannot determine that their truth conditions hold solely on the basis of our axioms and rules. On the other hand, since God is not an observable individual, then the truth or falsity of these statements cannot be determined by our observations either. These statements would not, then, belong to the domain of rational theology. To hold such a statement as true would be, as I suggested earlier, to entertain a nonrational belief. It is statements such as these which would constitute what has traditionally been called revealed theology.

When we turn to the language of revealed doctrines, the problem becomes less clear, since there is very little agreement even among theologians as to the nature of revelation itself. And perhaps the claims of emotive language, convictional language or disguised moral discourse are more easily justified here. Certainly there are emotive, convictional and moral elements in revealed theology. However, it was our purpose to investigate the possibility that even the language of revealed doctrines may be treated as descriptive discourse. There is a section in the *Summa Theologica* concerning the language of Holy Scripture which may serve as a fruitful starting point. The Angelic Doctor writes:

> The author of Holy Scripture is God in whose power it is to signify His meanings, not by words only (as man can do), but also by things themselves. So, whereas in every other science things are signified by words, this science has the property that the things signified by the words have themselves also a signification . . . that signification whereby words signify things belongs to the first sense, the historical or literal. This signification whereby things signified by words have themselves also a signification is called the spiritual sense, which is based on the literal, and presupposes it.[14]

Here St. Thomas is suggesting that in Holy Scripture there are two levels of signification. There are in Scripture statements about things, or events, in the common world disclosed to us in experience, and these statements have a historical, or literal, signification. At this level they are to be interpreted, I would imagine, as any historical statement. We shall call these statements the record of revelation. If these statements are to be taken in their literal, or historical sense, then they must be taken as descriptive statements and their truth value must be determined in the same manner as any historical statement. It is not, however, their truth or falsity which makes these statements a part of the record of revelation. As true statements, if in fact they are true, they belong to secular history. What places them within the record of revelation is that the events, or things, described in these statements are also taken as having a signification, and it is the signification of the things described in the record that constitutes the spiritual signification. In so far as revealed theology is concerned, then, the truth or falsity of these statements may be interesting, but not crucial for their inclusion in the record. We must allow for what Dante has called "beauteous fiction"[15] or H. W. Robinson, more appropriately in this context, the "ministry of illusion."[16] The sole justification for the inclusion of these statements within the record of revelation is the fact that the things, or events, described by the statements have a spiritual signification.

In order to see how things, or events, as well as words, can have a signification, let us look at the way in which things can function as signs. The emphasis in contemporary philosophy on the use of linguistic signs has, I fear, blinded us to the fact that most of our signs are not linguistic signs at all. Consider the following example: Suppose that, as you walked out the door this morning, you looked up at the sky and noticed a dark cloud. Immediately you returned inside, got your umbrella and raincoat. What would you have done? You would have been taking the dark cloud as a sign of rain; for you it signified rain. And you interpreted this sign in terms of a certain type of behavior—your returning and getting your umbrella and raincoat. Not a single linguistic sign entered into this chain of events. On the other hand, suppose that you, upon seeing the dark cloud, uttered this verbal prediction to someone near you: "It is going to rain." This would be an interpretation of the sign in terms of a verbal prediction. But in either case, the dark cloud signified for you rain and served as a promise, a promise of rain.

Again let us return to St. Thomas and see how the things described in the record of revelation signify. He continues:

> so far as the things of the Old Law signify the things of the new law, there is the allegorical sense; so far as the things done in Christ, or so far as the things which signify Christ, are signs of what we ought to do, there is the moral sense. But so far as they signify what relates to eternal glory, there is the anagogical sense.[17]

In this quote St. Thomas has listed three ways in which the things, or events, described in the record of revelation may have spiritual significance. First, there is what he calls the allegorical sense. The word "allegory" comes from two Greek words, "to speak" and "another." To give an allegory is literally to speak of another. Here the things of the Old Testament are taken as signifying, or speaking of, the things of the New Testament. The previous illustration of the dark cloud as a sign will, I think, be helpful here. Just as the dark cloud served as a promise of rain, so the things of the Old Testament are interpreted as promises of things to come in the New Testament. That this type of interpretation is not foreign to the Bible itself goes without saying. It is this pattern of promise and fulfillment which gives the Biblical narrative its dramatic continuity. The application of the term, "Messiah," or its Greek cognate, "Christ," to Jesus of Nazareth is the affirmation that in him the promises of the Old Testament are fulfilled. In fact, what appears to be the earliest affirmation of the Christian Church is: "Let all the house of Israel therefore know assuredly that God has made him both Lord and Christ, this Jesus whom you crucified" (*RSV*, Acts 2:36).

Secondly, there is what St. Thomas has called the moral sense of signification. Here the behavior of Jesus of Nazareth and the things which signify him are taken as signs of how we ourselves should behave. This is to give expression to Jesus' exhortation: "If any man will come after me let him take up his cross and follow me" (*RSV*, Matt. 16:24). Thirdly, there is what St. Thomas has called the anagogical sense. The word "anagogical" comes from the Greek verb, "to raise up." Dante interprets the use of the word, "anagogical," in this context as meaning "above the sense."[18] Here the things of the sensible world are taken as signifying not some future things in the world of common experience, as the allegorical, nor are they taken as signifying how we should act in this life, as the moral, but as signifying our eternal glory—that is, signifying something about God.

In the illustration which used the dark cloud as a sign, it was suggested that a sign may be interpreted either in terms of a certain type of behavior or in the form of a verbal prediction. Let us say that the behavioral interpretation of the signs of revelation constitute the Christian life. Since, however, we are concerned with religious language, it is the verbal interpretations which interest us. To give a verbal interpretation of the signs which are taken as promises is to prophesy. To give a verbal interpretation of the signs in the moral sense is to exhort, or to give moral imperatives. To give a verbal interpretation of the signs in an anagogical sense is to give the doctrines of revealed theology.

Neither the prophecies nor the exhortations are statements; for these verbal expressions do not function descriptively. In contrast to describing what *is* the case, a prophecy concerns what is *expected* to be the case and an exhortation what *ought* to be the case. I would like to maintain, however, that the anagogical verbal interpretations of the things, or events, described in the record of revelation, which I take to be the doctrines of revealed theology, do function descriptively; that is they are taken as statements describing something about God. If this is the case, then we must be able to say what kind of truth conditions are to be given for these doctrines.

There have been attempts to formulate truth conditions for revealed doctrines in terms of the afterlife of human beings. John Hick[19] refers to this as eschatological verification. It is the attempt to formulate for religious statements truth conditions that can be determined to hold or not to hold after death. If these conditions could be clearly formulated, then this would assure the descriptive character of revealed doctrines. There is, however, a serious difficulty in this technique. As Professor Blackstone[20] has pointed out, this is a question-begging technique, for it assumes that the notion of the afterlife of human beings is itself a descriptively meaningful notion. And this is precisely one of the things which is in question. It means that one must be able to give a consistent meaning for the notion of an afterlife solely in terms of the concepts which we use to describe the common world disclosed to us in experience. That one can do this is seriously questionable. I would not, however, like to rule out the possibility at this point. It is the purpose of this paper to outline another alternative, which, in contrast to Hick's, may be called divine verification.

In order to clarify this position let us once again return to the use of the dark cloud as a sign. Granted that neither your behavioral interpretation, nor your verbal interpretation of the dark cloud in the form of a prediction is a statement, still one can raise the question as to whether or not your interpretation is justified. If you interpreted the dark cloud as a sign of rain, the thing that would justify your interpretation would be the fact of rain—in other words, the fulfillment of the promise. And the verbal expression which states the fact which fulfills the promise should be a statement which is either true or false. If this were not the case, then one interpretation would be as justifiable as another and we would have no way of distinguishing the false prophet from the true prophet. We maintained that it was the Christian affirmation that the promises of the Old Testament were fulfilled in Jesus of Nazareth and the verbal expression which justifies these interpretations is: "Jesus is the Christ, or Messiah."

Likewise, even though exhortations are not statements, we can raise the question of their justification. The Christian is exhorted to "take up his cross and follow" because Jesus is Lord. But Jesus' lordship finds its justification in his Messiahship. And here again our justification for the moral interpretation rests upon the messianic office of Jesus. We must, then, raise the question whether or not the verbal expression "Jesus of Nazareth is the Messiah" is a statement. The only basis, it seems to me, upon which the allegorical and the moral interpretations can be justified is on the basis that this verbal expression is a statement and is true. But if it is a statement, then truth conditions must be given for it. These truth conditions cannot be given in terms of Jesus of Nazareth's meeting the stipulations in the promises, for it is he who determines which prophecies are justified and which not. That is, he in the end is used to distinguish the false prophet from the true prophet. Likewise the truth conditions cannot be given in terms of his meeting certain moral requirements, for it is he who justifies the moral exhortations of the Christian.

If Jesus of Nazareth is in fact the Messiah, then he has this office solely on the basis of God's approval. In the end the crux of the Christian revelation rests upon the reported voice which came from heaven upon the baptism of Jesus: "This is my beloved Son, with whom I am well pleased" (*RSV*, Matt. 3:17). In other words, the truth conditions for the statement, "Jesus is the Messiah," must ultimately be given in terms of God's approval of him for this role. To quote again from Peter's sermon in Acts, "God has made him both Lord and Christ." In fact, I would like to propose that all revealed doctrines, in so far as they are descriptive sentences, assert something about God's approvals and disapprovals, or his evaluations of the things of this world, and that their truth conditions must in the end be given in these terms. It is precisely because of this fact that they can be said to be revelations of the character of God. Is it not a person's approvals and disapprovals, or his evaluations, that reveal his character? So it is with God. It is for this reason that God's judgment plays an essential role in the Biblical revelation. The Divine Yes and the Divine No reveal the character of God. And it is these statements which give us what St. Thomas has called the anagogical interpretations of the things recorded in Scripture. Here the things are taken as signs of God's evaluations and thus a revelation of his character. And the revealed doctrines are true in so far as they state what are, in fact, God's evaluations and false in so far as they do not.

Throughout this analysis of revealed theology we have, of course, assumed that the rational theologian has succeeded in his task and given us a descriptive meaning for the term, "God." Likewise, we have assumed that he has been able to define the various traditional attributes of omnipresence, omniscience, omnipotence, and goodness, or perfection. But if we are to give meaning to the verbal expressions of revealed theology, then the rational theologian must also be able to give descriptive meaning to the notion of God's evaluation of the world. In other words, he must be able, in terms of God's goodness, or perfection, to give a definition for the expression, "X is more valuable to God than Y." Of course, if the task of rational theology is an impossible task, then the verbal expressions of revealed theology, as well as the verbal expressions of rational theology, are descriptively meaningless. In this way revelation is dependent upon reason—that is, for its meaningfulness. There are good indications, however, that the task of rational theology is not an impossible one.

For the purposes of our discussion, however, let us assume once again that this task has been accomplished. It seems obvious that a statement of the form, "X is more valuable to God than Y," cannot be determined to be either true or false on the basis of human observation. At least it is not at all clear what sort of observations are called for. Also, a statement of the form, "X is more valuable to God than Y" could not be shown to be necessarily true; that is, we could not determine its truth value by appealing to our rules and axioms. This can be indicated by comparing a statement of this form to a statement of the form, "God knows X." Now if omniscience has been defined, then to be known by God would be a universal property of all individuals. In fact, this is precisely what omniscience means. Consequently, a statement of the form, "God knows X," no matter what X might be, would be necessarily true. On the other hand, to be more valuable to God than something else could not possibly be a universal property and, consequently, could not be proven of any individual. This means, then, that to accept as true any statement concerning God's evaluations of the world is to entertain what I have previously called a non-rational belief, for it is technologically beyond the power of human beings to determine by a rational methodology whether or not its truth conditions do in fact hold. God alone could verify the statement.

Thus it seems that we are left with a set of non-rational beliefs, those beliefs about God's evaluations of the world, which cannot be justified by a rational methodology. Yet these beliefs, it would seem, should determine to a large extent our attitude toward life and the world and have serious consequences for our actions. But these are beliefs which can only be accepted or rejected on the basis of faith. The status of theological beliefs suggested here is perhaps best expressed by Socrates in his closing remarks to the judges who had just voted to condemn him to death: "The hour of departure has arrived, and we go our ways —I to die, and you to live. Which is better God only knows." But I hasten to add: if God does know then, that makes a difference, for it makes revealed theology possible.

Notes

1. Austin Farrar, *Faith and Logic*, ed. Basil Mitchell (London: George Allen and Unwin, 1957), p. 9.

2. Ibid., p. 9.

3. Ibid., p. 10.

4. See A. J. Ayer, *Language, Truth and Logic* (London: Victor Gollancz, 1946).

5. See R. B. Braithwaite, *An Empiricist's View of the Nature of Religious Belief* (Cambridge: Cambridge University Press, 1955).

6. See Willem Zuurdeeg, *An Analytical Philosophy of Religion* (New York: Abingdon, 1958).

7. See *Summa Theologica,* I,q 1,a 1. All quotations from the *Summa Theologica* are taken from the Anton C. Pegis revision of the English Dominican translation in *Basic Writings of Saint Thomas Aquinas* (New York: Random House, 1945).

8. St. Anselm, *Proslogium,* ed. Sidney Nortan Deane (Lasalle, Illinois: Open Court, 1958), p. 8.

9. Ibid., p. 154.

10. This is somewhat unfair to St. Anselm, for he does suggest the conception of an omnipresent individual in his *Reply to Guanilon.* See ibid., p. 155.

11. *Summa Theologica,* I,q 2,a 3.

12. Frank Harrison, "Some Brief Remarks Concerning the *Quinque Viae* of Saint Thomas," *Franciscan Studies* 21 (1961): 85.

13. Ibid., p. 80.

14. *Summa Theologica,* I,q 1,a 10.

15. Dante, "First Treatise," *The Convico,* ed. Philip H. Wickstead (London: J. M. Dent, 1940), p. 63 (1. 25).

16. H. W. Robinson, *Inspiration and Revelation in the Old Testament* (Oxford: Clarendon Press, 1946), p. 45.

17. *Summa Theologica,* I,q 1,a 10.

18. Dante, "First Treatise," p. 64 (1. 52).

19. See, for example, John Hick, *Philosophy of Religion* (Englewood Cliffs: Prentice–Hall, 1963), pp. 100–103.

20. William T. Blackstone, *The Problem of Religious Knowledge* (Englewood Cliffs: Prentice–Hall, 1963), p. 114.

CAN THERE BE PROOFS FOR THE EXISTENCE OF GOD?

Charles Hartshorne

This is an essay in "natural theology," that is to say, theology through the reason which is inherent in man's nature and without benefit of grace or "special" revelation. It is a doctrine of the Roman Catholic Church that natural theology is possible and that, without this possibility, revelation would lose its reasonableness. Although I am not a Romanist, I honor the theologians who have steadily maintained this tenet through the centuries of discredit into which natural theology has passed since Hume and Kant.

However, we do live in a different age, and if we are to find a basis in reason for religion it cannot be in so simple a way as that of the great founders of the metaphysics of religion.

My first suggestion is that although natural theology does not argue from revealed premises, it may quite properly allow revelation to suggest what the topic for consideration is to be. It may allow revealed religion, or what claims to be such, to furnish the question, even though not the answer. Here I am apparently saying the opposite of what Tillich says. I am saying that revelation defines the question, while philosophy, or secular reason, gives the answer. If the task is to form a rational theory about the central religious idea, the idea of God, it seems proper to begin by asking religion, including revealed religion, what it means by "God." For if natural theology is not to support belief in the God who is worshipped, why speak of "theology" at all? "Theos" is basically a religious word.

If God is the one who is worshipped, what is worship? Tillich profoundly argues that the Great Commandment to love God with all one's being amounts to a definition at once of worship and of the term God. Whatever can be loved in integral fashion, that is, can be worshipped, is God. I take this to be the proper way to use the term. Any description of God incompatible with this requirement is a misuse of words, a changing of the subject. I believe that Spinoza's description of his deity was in some features incompatible with his claim to worship that deity. But the issues here are subtle, and I must continue.

In my opinion the great theologians and philosophers of our tradition were primarily (in one way or another) guilty unconsciously of changing the subject and misusing the word God. They identified deity with the wholly absolute, infinite, or eternal. But worship as such does not imply this, and indeed, I hold, is incompatible with it. No one can love the mere absolute with all his being. He cannot even love it with all his intellectual being; for intellect is concerned with the relative and the changing, as well as with the absolute or immutable. In Augustine's essay on Free Will one sees clearly the strange notion that the mathematician as such is peculiarly close to God, which implies that the historian, or anyone concerned with historical processes, must be very far from Him. Numbers, for Augustine, are close to God because they are immutable; it follows that people, who are highly changeable, must be far from God. This may be rather typical Greek philosophy, but what has it to do with Jewish or Christian or Islamic religion? No one today thinks that the mathematician, as compared, say, to the theoretical physicist, is peculiarly godlike. And what about the poor historian? Is he looking straight away from deity?

We are no longer Greeks in philosophy. We realize that immutability may only mean utter abstractness. Numbers are immutable because they are so little, not because they are so much. In their concrete use, to explain actual processes, numbers are invaluable instruments, but merely in themselves they are only superb intellectual toys, and it is not in *their* direction primarily that we must seek the greatest of all realities.

Omniscience and omnipotence, viewed through Greek spectacles as wholly immutable, generate antinomies, which some take as occasions for awe and intellectual humility. But humility and awe are not the same as love, and cannot alone fulfill the great commandment. The tortures which religious people have long endured through trying to reconcile purely eternal knowledge, or the omnipotence of a wholly absolute being, with the freedom of our temporal acts, or with the occurrence of suffering and other forms of evil, have often been downright masochistic. And

I do not think they have a proper place in genuine love of God.

How then is God to be described, beyond saying that he is the one to be worshipped? On the one hand, if there are limits to God's perfection, or if he depends upon others for his worth, he cannot, it seems, merit worship. Can "unconditional" devotion have a "conditioned" terminus or ground? asks Tillich. So he infers the unconditionedness of God from the definition of worship. But this is either an extremely vague or ambiguous use of words, or else it is just the old Greek error against which I, and not only I, have long been protesting. For whether one says "absolute" or "unconditioned" is of no consequence, since the clear meaning, if any, is the same. And "immutable" is implied in either case. Is our love for God immutable? Moreover, no one interested, as we are bound to be, in history, in change, can possibly love the immutable with *all* his being. Only by self-deception can he suppose himself to do this.

Yet, on the other hand, if one gives up terms like absolute, infinite, or immutable altogether in describing God, does that not also conflict with worship? Can we, without reservation, devote ourselves to serving One whose knowledge or goodness is defective, or in whom *everything* is subject to alteration? The church fathers, the classical theologians generally, had excellent reasons for supposing that absoluteness, infinity, and eternity must *somehow* apply to the divine. What they failed to see was that relativity, finitude, and change, for equally good reasons, must also apply and that the task of reason in theology is to reconcile the two sets of requirements, not to give monopolistic privileges to one or the other. I have shown, in various writings (for instance, in *The Divine Relativity*), that this reconciliation is possible or, at least, that no obvious contradiction results. And the claim has not, so far, been refuted.

We now come to the key question of natural theology: taking God to have both infinity and finitude, both absoluteness and relativity, both eternity and alterability, each in just the fashion required by the definition of worship, what can reason say as to the reality of the deity thus defined? Here we face an old topic, the theistic proofs. Hume, Kant, and others are supposed to have demolished these, once for all. And theologians have sometimes said good riddance. There are, however, some flaws in this conception of intellectual history.

First Hume and, even more, Kant were imprisoned in the Greek bias which tended to identify eternity, infinity, absoluteness, with divinity. This presupposition plays a decisive role in their conception of the proofs. And indeed, the objection to the identification of God with the absolute is not only that it changes the subject from the God of worship to something else (really a philosophical idol), but also that the notion of a purely absolute, infinite, and eternal reality is riddled with antinomies, if taken as anything but an abstraction wholly incapable of existing save as an element in something more concrete. Any alleged proof for so illogical a conclusion must be equally illogical. Therefore, the failure of the classical proofs as they stand is indeed good riddance. But only because they were proofs, not for God, but for an idolatrous absurdity.

Second, Hume and Kant argued against natural theology from premises which not only begged the question, but are today highly controversial. The Newtonian world picture was implicitly antitheistic, and to argue from it was to prejudge the theological issue. Accordingly, the collapse of this world picture reopens and recasts the fundamental questions of natural theology. Many philosophers heap scorn upon theologians who find evidences for God in quantum mechanics. But they are missing the main point, which is that Newtonian physics, taken literally, as it was usually, though wrongly, taken, implies the *un*reality of God. A cosmic engineer is not God; it cannot be loved with all one's being, not even if the engineer is said to make the material with which he works. A world-machine, a pseudo-concept at best, could not be a divine creation. The view of the world as essentially machine-like was, to be sure, no result of scientific inquiry, but an unlimited extrapolation such as only philosophy could possibly justify. And no philosophy could justify it either, for it was an internally incoherent doctrine, as Peirce, Bergson, Whitehead, and others have shown. We may well rejoice that we are rid of this incubus. But the consequences for religious metaphysics have yet to be widely appreciated. Cultural lag is greater in philosophy than in any other subject, even though in no subject, perhaps, is there so much anticipation of cultural developments.

A third weakness of Hume's and Kant's alleged refutation of the possibility of theistic proofs is the lack of an adequate understanding, such as is possible today, of what it means to try to "prove" a philosophical doctrine. Hume and Kant themselves offer proofs for various philosophical contentions of their own; however, like all proofs outside of formal logic, finite arithmetic, and pure geometry, these Humian and Kantian proofs rely upon premises which are open to controversy. And indeed, if the alleged impossibility of theistic proofs only means that any such proof must have more or less controversial premises, then theism may be in no worse case than any other philosophical view. To draw the conclusion that the divine existence is a mere matter of faith is to imply that the whole of philosophy is a mere matter of faith. And this is scarcely what Hume and Kant intended. Some contemporary philosophers who reject natural theology may perhaps be willing to accept such a radical conclusion. Thus Wittgenstein says that philosophizing, as he practices it, makes no assertions—and, I suppose, no denials. Even so, would he want to say that theoretical reason is in no sense operative in philosophy?

In view of the three weaknesses listed above, I maintain that Hume and Kant proved nothing for or against the possibility of rational grounds for theistic belief. (1) They changed the subject from the God of religion to a philosophical idol of absoluteness; (2) they reasoned from question-begging and, as we can see today, highly dubious premises; and (3) they had an inadequate grasp of what can be meant by rational argument in philosophy. Have contemporary philosophical critics of natural theology overcome these defects? I am not aware that they have. Mostly they rely upon Hume and Kant, with casual emendations, elaborations, or extensions.

But perhaps contemporary *theological* critics of the claims of natural theology to prove the existence of God have shown their illegitimacy? I cannot see this either. It is not enough to appeal to the fall of man and the corruption of human reason. Such ideas are too vague to be decisive, even if one grants that from the standpoint of a certain revelation they are to be accepted. Theologians too are under the fall, even when they reason about natural theology, or anything else. Appeal to such a blanket defect can hardly illuminate definite issues very much.

Schweitzer and also Brunner argue that theoretical reason is bound to go astray when confronting nature and human life, with their mixtures of good and evil, of realized ideals and frustrations. Must not the dilemma always arise: *either* explain away the evils by a false idealization of reality *or* deny the perfection of divine power and goodness? However, the answer is that, in fact we have had philosophers who have done neither of these things. Nor is there any logical necessity for doing either. If "perfection" is used in the religiously appropriate sense, God's perfect power and goodness need not imply that the evils in the world must be his doing. There is therefore no forced option between denying divine power or goodness and denying the reality of evil. In short, this argument against the power of reason to deal with religious questions is fallacious. It is an illicit generalization from an oversimplified view of the history of philosophy and of the logic of certain concepts.

It is time we came to grips with the question of proofs, that is, rational grounds for belief. In a formal proof a set of premises, which we may put into a single complex premise p, logically entails a conclusion q. So we reason "p, therefore q." To this it is always possible to reply, "I do not accept p, hence—so far as the argument goes—I need not accept q." The old-fashioned idea, however, was that in *some* cases this way out is impossible, since p is in those cases self-evident and undeniable. But through the centuries we have learned the hard way that strictly undeniable premises are scarce, particularly undeniable premises having controversial conclusions. In this sense, it may well be impossible to prove the existence of God, if "proof" means valid reasoning from premises that only an utter blockhead or dishonest person could deny. But then would not every philosophically interesting doctrine also turn out to be unprovable? And if this means that there is no scope for reason in the subject perhaps we philosophers should have the grace to stop pretending and go out of business!

The value of a formal proof is not that it establishes its conclusion for every man, no matter what his assumptions and attitudes, but that it establishes a logical price for rejecting a certain conclusion. If the conclusion does follow from the premise, the minimal logical price of rejecting the conclusion is rejecting the premise. Of those who question the conclusion, some will already be aware of this price, and be willing to pay it; some will not be aware of it but, upon learning that it is the price, will find themselves just as able to reject the premise as the conclusion; but finally, some who have *not* previously understood the price of unbelief will feel this price to be so high that they will want to reconsider the matter. And then suppose that they can be shown that still other premises entail the conclusion, and suppose they find the rejection of these other premises likewise difficult, so that the logical price of unbelief comes to appear to them far higher than they at first suspected—can anyone deny that this *might* suffice to turn unbelief into belief?

If a valid proof is thus one which, for some persons at least, makes the logical price of unbelief appear unbearably high, then I am confident that there can be theistic proofs. And I hold that they can be of great importance, so that, on this issue, the Roman Catholic Church is to be congratulated on its steadiness and courage. I take the theistic proofs, properly stated and fairly evaluated, to be as intellectually respectable as philosophical arguments are likely to be, and I am not yet ready to admit that this is not saying anything. I also think, however, that the traditional statements, and traditional evaluations, of the proofs are mostly careless, sloppy, or unfair. In no portion of their responsibility, perhaps, have members of my profession done so poorly as in this one. Historical reasons for this cannot be gone into here. Some of them have already been hinted at.

The time has come for some examples of theistic proof. The logical price of denying the reality of God can be exhibited in various ways, each of which can be put in the form of a dilemma, or better still, a trilemma. For instance, if theism is defended by saying: the world is orderly, order implies an orderer, the only conceivable orderer for a world is God, then the unbeliever is by implication doing one or more of the following: denying that there is order in the world, denying that order implies an orderer, or denying that the power to order a world implies divinity. Of course there are those who are ready to make one or more of these denials. But the three propositions in question can be so presented as to make their denial seem counter-intuitive to some of us. For us, the argument is a valid one. This is all that any philosophical argument accomplishes, when you "get right down to it."

Let us outline the argument in more detail. (1) A simply unordered world is a contradiction in terms; it is no object of possible knowledge and there is no way to distinguish it clearly from nothing at all, (2) order among existing individuals means some unitary influence or power acting upon those individuals; finally, (3) only power superior in principle to ordinary powers, only divine power, could constitute the cosmic orderer.

It is irrelevant to point out that there is disorder in the world as well as order. For, in the first place, we are not asking how can there be perfect cosmic order, but only how can there be anything but cosmic chaos, anything but unthinkable confusion. And in the second place, to say that order consists in a superior power influencing all other powers is not only different from saying that the superior power is the only power, a sheer monopoly, it is even incompatible with saying this. "Omnipotence" as a pure monopoly of power or decision-making is a pseudo-concept, and has nothing to do with the argument we are discussing. And only this pseudo-concept implies that the world-order must or could be absolute, free from any elements of disorder or partial chaos. As Hume and Kant failed to see, the supreme power cannot be the sole power, for then "supreme" would have no meaning. Also, if there is a multiplicity of powers, and if a "power" which fails to influence any effect is meaningless, then the total cosmic effect cannot be determined by the supreme power alone. Even supreme power can only impose limits on the disagreements, conflicts, or confusions among lesser powers; it cannot simply eliminate these confusions, for this would require its becoming the sole power, and this is nonsense. Power acts upon power, not upon the powerless. Activity and passivity belong together; what cannot act cannot be acted upon, and what cannot be acted upon cannot act. Both God and the creatures must influence reality as a whole, and there must be mutual influence between God and creatures. I cannot here further defend these principles.

We must move on. Why not, some would say, suppose that there can be order even without an ordering power? This would mean that a multitude of individuals, by blind chance, necessity, or deliberate intention, cooperated to produce or maintain a world order. Cooperation does occur, for instance, in the work of a committee. But the first act of cooperation is to choose a chairman, if one has not already been provided in the act of setting up the committee. Also the committee must have been

given a directive from someone, if it is to know what its cooperation is to be about. In politics, which is the high-level obvious
case best known in our experience, it is the "rule of one" which
alone enables chaos to be avoided. If there is not a ruler, he must
be created, even though his rule is narrowly limited in time,
function, or both, and though he may be called chairman or
president, not ruler. But the ability to cooperate enough to
choose a ruler presupposes a more basic order, and this order
must be traced back either to previous acts of influential individuals persuading the rest into a decent degree of conformity,
or to "laws of nature." Now the laws of nature are the very
question at issue, not an explanation. Political laws we understand, we know how they originate and in what they consist;
but how there can be laws of nature is the riddle we seek to un-
ravel. The political analogy has not been shown to be irrelevant
or absurd, provided it is properly formulated. The ultimate principles are: (a) order is explained by the influence of one upon
many; (b) this influence in turn implies some sort of superiority
of the one to the many; and (c) the possibility of universal or
cosmic ordering implies a universal superiority such as is clearly
conceivable only through the idea of divinity.

I believe that the foregoing outline could be strengthened by
developing various lines of collateral reasoning. But I wish in-
stead to present another theistic proof. This is the ethical proof.
In ethics we need to assume that, taking their consequences into
account, some modes of action are better than others. For if
right ways of acting do not, in general at least, produce better
consequences than wrong ways, what is the point of right and
wrong? But consequences may be divided into immediate or
short run and more or less remote or long run. Both are in principle relevant. If it were the case that doing good to my neighbor
now must result in his greater misery later on, or if doing good
to my children must result to a greater extent in misery for my
grandchildren, how in either case could I feel obligated to do the
more immediate good? But on the other hand, how much do we
know about the long-run effects of our acts? We and every subsequent generation will presumably die in the end; and the human race itself will eventually perish, or at least will change
beyond any knowable limit, and beyond any definitely traceable
benefit from our individual actions. How, in all this, can we un-

derstand a long-run outcome of our nobler and wiser actions which will be definitely better than the long-run outcome of our most unkind, cowardly, or foolish ones? In the grave, what will it matter? Or, is it the fate of posterity through an infinity of millennia which we should be concerned with? Since we cannot possibly have any definite knowledge, or even imagining, of such an infinity of human survival, our basic ethical notion of ultimate consequences seems to vanish into total indefiniteness.

Here then is the argument. Admitted that the aim of life is the service of God, and that the long-run good we accomplish is our contribution to the divine "glory" (in the old and perhaps unnecessarily mysterious language), then neither our own death nor the ultimate fate of humanity can prevent us from having done better by acting nobly and wisely than by acting ignobly and foolishly. For it is not perishable generations we are seeking ultimately to serve but imperishable deity; it is not a forgetful and perhaps foolish posterity, or a humanity after immeasurable changes, on this changing planet or elsewhere, that we hope finally to benefit, but a divine life definitely able to cherish with adequate wisdom each transient beauty of human experience in everlasting remembrance. Deny such a divine cherishing and remembrance and what becomes of the idea that right actions have better consequences than wrong ones? The unbeliever faces a trilemma: (1) the short-run human consequences; or (2) the long-run consequences for the human race (or all sentient creatures); or (3) the long-run consequences for individuals conceived as surviving death forever. One or more of these must constitute the ultimate value of our behavior. The first proposal (short-run consequences only) seems to destroy any genuine rationality in ethics; the second and the third (the immortality of the species or the individual) must remain wholly indeterminate for human knowledge. This is a part of the price of nonbelief, that there can be no positive rational aim, intelligible as such. The service of God, on the contrary, is positive, rational, and, for the believer, intelligible. For the unbeliever, there can only be a vague hope that somehow something good, we know not what, will in the long run ensue from our efforts.

This argument, too, has been poorly presented in the literature; indeed, it is so little known as to have scarcely been evaluated at all, even unfairly. Usually the contribution to ethics accredited to belief has been in the form of "sanctions," heavenly rewards and hellish punishments, a lamentable business of contradictorily asking us to act from love of others and of God, while yet telling us that unless it is possible to act rightly from desire of self-advantage or fear of self-disadvantage, we cannot be expected to act rightly at all. Sanctions can only be needed for the unethical, but then at most hell alone, and not heaven, could be relevant! This way of arguing for God I wholly repudiate. (Kant's form of ethical argument was more subtle, but still unsatisfactory.)

God is needed, not so that there can be human advantage in the ultimate long run for good acts and human disadvantage in the long run for bad acts, but so that the *ultimate human* long run need not concern us at all, but only the human present and *relative* long run (which alone we have any power to know). Our need is not for an ultimate aim of self-advantage, or human advantage, but for an ultimate aim—period. If people can sometimes do things out of love for children or posterity rather than concern for their own futures, then still more can they do things for God, who alone is wholly lovable, and whose future alone is secure from death and corrupting change. To suppose that in doing things for God we must be motivated finally by concern for our human futures is to imply that God is less lovable even than human beings! This only brings into the open how little some men have understood what worship of God is all about.

Besides the fixation on sanctions, the other chief reason why the proof from the necessity for a rational aim has been largely overlooked is the fixation on "the absolute" (or "unconditioned") as the very definition of deity. Of course one cannot bestow benefits upon "the absolute," the wholly immutable or infinite. So much the worse for this definition of God, which makes "serving" him at best a deceptive disguise for the creatures' service of themselves and one another. A "glory of God" which it can be our aim to promote cannot be simply absolute; for the merely absolute or unconditioned is not possibly promoted, enriched, enhanced, furthered—in plain English, it is not served in any reasonable sense whatever.

It should scarcely need saying that every legitimate aim which an unbeliever can have, such as promoting human happiness, is included in the aim of serving God. For what benefit can we bestow upon the divine except by realizing in our life, and favoring in the lives of other creatures, the actualization of such values as our—and their—inborn constitutions make possible? As Hume said so well, there is nothing of value we could possibly offer God except human (or creaturely) happiness. If our humility or "obedience" serves God it can only be because it is required for creaturely happiness or welfare. To say otherwise is to put God on the level of tyrants, basically insecure rulers, who need to be reassured as to the status of their preeminence. The "good life for man or other creatures" is then also man's only gift to God. But all of it is such a gift. Hence the humanistic objectives are entirely embraced in theistic religion.

I have outlined two arguments illustrating the logical price of unbelief. There are at least four others of comparable power. There is an argument from truth, or from the idea of knowledge, which I call the epistemic or idealistic argument—the latter because it is chiefly idealists who have developed it, especially Josiah Royce, though they failed, I think, to put it into a wholly correct form. There is an aesthetic argument, from the idea of beauty or harmony of experience as implying harmony in the inclusive object of experience. There is the cosmological argument from the contingency of the world, which Hume and Kant mis-stated and, in my opinion, did not really refute. There is finally the ontological argument invented, but not adequately analyzed, by Anselm, and essentially misunderstood by all of its famous critics, as I claim to have shown in two books. The ontological argument confronts us with a trilemma: (1) The idea of God lacks consistent cognitive meaning (the positivistic position); (2) The idea of God has consistent meaning, and what it describes exists, but only in fact, not by any a priori necessity; (3) The idea of God has consistent meaning, but what it describes in fact fails to exist.

1. The greatest difficulty confronting the Anselmian is to disprove the first or positivistic horn of the trilemma. Here Anselm was weakest, though it is just here that critics generally fail to attack him. But notice that if positivism is correct, then theism *could not* be true, for a question can have an answer only if the question makes sense. Kant failed to see that if he really refuted the argument, he also refuted theism itself. Here I agree with J. N. Findlay.

2. That God exists in mere fact, not by a priori necessity, would indeed mean that the ontological inference is fallacious. For only what is a priori can be formally proved. But Anselm really did show, as I have argued in many writings, that to exist contingently, or so that non-existence would have been possible, is to exist as other than divine. Only that which could not conceivably fail to exist can be unsurpassable or worthy of worship, and only that which is unsurpassable could not conceivably fail to exist.

3. If God could not exist contingently, or in mere fact, he also could not contingently fail to exist. The question, then, is not an empirical one at all, but in the broad sense logical, a question of meaning. The non-existence of unsurpassability can only mean its inconceivability. Against this positivistic alternative one can object: (a) If there is a contradiction, let it be pointed out. (b) The capacity of the idea of God to explicate the meaning of cosmic order, the meaning of a rational aim in ethics, and to solve other categorical problems, seems incompatible with its being without cognitive import. In this way the other theistic proofs strengthen the ontological at its weakest point, the assumption of consistent meaning. At the same time, and without vicious circularity, the ontological proof can strengthen the other proofs at *their* weakest points. For, these proofs start with categories which seem required to deal with basic human problems, and so their meaning and consistency can reasonably be assumed, but without the ontological proof one might look upon theism as merely one among competing explanations of basic features of reality. The ontological proof, however, shows that there can be no competing explanations, since if the theistic explanation is genuinely conceivable it must be uniquely true. Thus this proof shows that no issue of empirical fact can be involved, but only necessities of meaning. If theism is logically tenable, it is true; if it is not true, then it is somehow illogical and could not be true, no matter what may or may not be observed in any experience.

I believe, however, that any of the proofs, adequately developed, will by itself give good support to the same conclusion as the others, and that the premises of all the proofs would be intuitively convincing if we could think clearly enough. Weak and strong points in the proofs are ultimately subjective or psychological matters. Even the distinction between the proofs is due to lack of clarity in our thinking. Either theism is rational and necessarily true, and all competing theories irrational and necessarily false, or theism is irrational and could not be true. Proofs are but ways of trying to exhibit the *unique rationality of theism* as a metaphysical doctrine. And in my judgment the greater burden of proof is in any case not upon theism. The fruitful attitude in all knowledge is not to ask for proof, but to ask for disproof. Popper's emphasis upon falsification is to the point. When Kant said that God could neither be proved nor disproved, he ought to have asked himself, what can it mean to say that a doctrine, against which there could be no evidence, yet might be false? If *we* could not know the non-existence of God, who could? Obviously God Himself could not know his own non-existence. And if this non-existence could not be known by anyone, is it not a meaningless notion? But then either theism is necessarily true or positivism is so, and in the latter case, there is no room for faith. Faith is senseless unless truth is at least possible. I hold that the divine non-existence is not a logically legitimate notion and that everyone who is unwilling to espouse the positivistic denial of meaning to theism ought to accept its truth.

The believer need only be sure of one thing, that his belief is not absurd. And if it is absurd, then so, it seems, is the idea of rational ethics, or of a value to human life from the standpoint of the ultimate long run. And then what is not absurd? The existentialists unwittingly support the theistic argument by terming life itself an absurdity. For in that case, any belief is as good as any other, for belief expresses life and cannot do anything else. I find it incomparably more reasonable to suppose that life and belief in the cosmic harmonizer of life and summator of its achievements are alike free from essential absurdity.

RELIGIOUS DISCOURSE AND MYTH*

Robert H. Ayers

In recent years, scholars in a wide variety of disciplines have written learned treatises which purported to shed light on the nature of myth and mythical thinking in human experience. These scholars have included social-anthropologists, classicists, philosophers, and theologians. Even a superficial perusal of the literature in the field reveals a bewildering variety of meaning attached to the word "myth." Indeed, this word seems to be one of the most widely traveled semantic hobos of our times. This would be confusing enough in itself, but confusion is added to confusion by the fact that any one author may use the word ambiguously and equivocally within one work.

It would be presumptuous of me to think that by means of a brief essay I could produce clarity in an area which has been researched by so many distinguished scholars and yet in which so much confusion abounds. Apparently, an enormous amount of effort in careful and critical research and analysis on the part of many scholars would be required to accomplish this task. My task in this essay involves three items. (1) I will attempt to make as clear as possible the sense in which I use the word "myth"; (2) I will try to justify in so far as possible the use of this sense of the word; and (3) In the major portion of my discussion, I will inquire as to the relevance, if any, of this sense of the word to religious discourse. Item three will contain three sections. (a) I will try to make clear what I mean by "religious discourse"; (b) I will discuss the positions of some contemporary theologians with regard to myth and religious discourse; and (c) I will draw some conclusions with regard to the relevance of myth for religious discourse.

*This essay appeared in somewhat different form as "'Myth' and Theological Discourse: A Profusion of Confusion," *Anglican Theological Review* 48 (April 1966): 200–217.

1. The Meaning of "Myth"

It is doubtful that this notorious hobo, "myth," can ever be settled in a permanent abode in ordinary usage. However, it may be possible to provide him with at least a legal residence to which he may be returned from time to time to gain some degree of stability and definiteness. Such a residence will not prove very helpful if it is selected with complete arbitrariness and contains no features similar to his other places of abode. That is to say, the meaning of myth I propose to use will be stipulative in the sense that it is not a report of the dictionary definition. Yet it is not an arbitrary stipulation based solely on personal whim. Its formulation has been influenced by some contemporary research on myth in the history of religion.

The definition proposed here is simply this: "myth" is a value-charged story expressing to some degree the life orientation of a group and/or individual. It seems to me that the three defining characteristics involved in this definition, namely (1) a value-charged story, (2) expressing to some degree, and (3) the life orientation of a group and/or individual, provide the word "myth" with a designation or intension which is adequate for its denotation or extension. I believe that the word so defined does not exclude from its area of denotation those things which traditionally have been labeled myths, nor does it include too much. Rather it emphasizes a feature which for the most part has been overlooked until recent times—a feature which broadens somewhat the scope of the word's designation and denotation.

2. Justification of the Proposed Definition and Use of "Myth"

An analysis of the definitions of myth given in Webster's *Third New International Dictionary* will help to clarify by way of contrast what is involved in our proposed definition. The three definitions given are as follows: "(1) a story that is usually of unknown origin and at least partially traditional, that ostensibly relates historical events usually of such character as to explain some practice, belief, institution or natural phenomenon, and that is especially associated with religious rites and beliefs; (2) a story invented as a veiled explanation of a truth; (3) a person or thing existing only in imagination or whose actuality is not verifiable."[1]

Let us consider certain key terms and phrases in these definitions, namely, "explanation," "invented," "existing only in imagination," and "actuality is not verifiable." These terms and phrases suggest that the author made the following assumptions: (1) myth is primarily a conceptual phenomenon; (2) myth fails to pass the tests for truth established in current scientific methodology; (3) since it fails to pass the tests, myth is necessarily a false story. I think it can be shown that these assumptions are questionable.

First, it is highly questionable that the primary purpose and function of myth-making and telling is to satisfy man's intellectual curiosity. This is not to say that in myth-making and telling, man's thought processes are not involved. This would be absurd, but it is equally as absurd to imply that this is all that is involved. Myth involves one as a total person—a thinking, willing, and feeling being.

Studies of ancient cultures have shown that it is a mistake to suppose that explanation was a primary feature of their myths. As a matter of fact, it may be suspected that such a supposition represents a blind spot on the part of those who hold it—a blind spot which arises from the presupposition that ancient man was simply a more naive version of contemporary man. Several contemporary scholars[2] have come to the conclusion that the major feature of the myths of ancient cultures was not that of explaining certain things but that of participating in certain realities as these realities were understood. Eliade, for example, on the basis of his studies comes to the conclusion that "myth is not just an infantile or aberrant creation of 'primitive' humanity, but is the expression of a mode of being in the world. . . . Myths reveal the structure of reality . . . [and] are the exemplary models for human behavior."[3] For those who believe them, myths give expression to that which is held to be most important and most real even though observation may not be able to establish some details of the story as real in the factual sense.

In using the term "expression" I do not mean to imply that all that was involved was "telling" or "instruction." Rather, involved in this expression was participation in the realities which were held to be most important. As Thomas J. J. Altizer has pointed out, "myth is not basically a literary or conceptual category. Myth is a primary mode of the religious response which in

its origin cannot be separated from ritual. . . . [It is] a mode of encounter with the sacred . . . [and is] action as well as word."[4]

In light of these studies, it is clearly a mistake to emphasize
explanation as the chief feature of myths and then to assume that
they were primarily conceptual in nature. This is to make a defining characteristic of an accompanying characteristic and thus
to restrict too narrowly the area of denotation. It is true, of
course, that explanatory elements are sometimes present in
myths. Some myths do contain elements of what we might call
"primitive science," but these are contingently accompanying
features, sometimes present and sometimes absent. The contemporary studies cited justify us in using the term "myth" to label
those value-charged stories expressing the life orientation of a
group and/or individual whether these stories do or do not contain elements of explanation or primitive science.

The second and third assumptions presupposed in the definitions given in Webster are closely interrelated. Myths are viewed
as false because some elements of some myths do not pass the
truth tests of twentieth-century scientific methodology. At least
three comments are relevant here. (1) To hold that myths are
fanciful stories is to assume that they were and are lightly regarded by those who accept them. This is not the case. For
those both past and present who believe them, myths refer to that
which is for them the actual meaning and value of human and
cosmic reality. As William F. Zuurdeeg has pointed out, to the
committed Nazi, "the myth of the Aryan race and of Blut and
Boden (blood and soil) expressed an idea that was precious for
the believers, the most real, the most profound meaning of life."[5]
(2) To hold that myths are false stories (which apparently is the
popular view of myths) is to rule out of consideration as myths
those stories to which truth-criteria cannot be applied either because we do not as yet have the knowledge whereby we can in
practice apply these criteria or because it is logically impossible
for us as human beings to apply these criteria. (3) To hold that
myths are false stories assumes a value-judgment concerning the
scientific methodology of our times—that such methodology is
absolute and unchanging. This is not the case, for any superficial
investigation of cultural history reveals the changes that occur
from time to time with respect to the methods of distinguishing
fact from fancy, truth from falsity. It would be presumptuous in-

deed to claim that the methodology of the present will be that of the future. Thus we would have to wait until tomorrow to find out whether what we took to be true today were myths or not. Such an absurd consequence is avoided, of course, if we refuse to define myth in terms of false stories. The definition which we have proposed, namely, that myth is a value-charged story expressing to some degree the life orientation of a group and/or individual, provides us with a means of distinguishing myth from non-myth whatever the scientific methodology of a culture may be. If myths are false, they are false not because they are myths but for the same reasons that anything else is considered to be false.

In light of this examination of the denial by some contemporary scholars of the assumptions involved in the popular definitions of myth, I think our definition of myth has been justified, at least to some degree. Twentieth-century studies have denied that myth is a purely intellectual phenomenon arising out of curiosity; so I have used the words "life orientation," implying thereby that myth involves the whole person in his understanding of life's direction and purpose. Twentieth-century studies have denied that myth is primarily concerned with explanation; so I have used the word "expression" indicating that this involves one in participating in what is believed to be one's life orientation. Twentieth-century studies have denied that myths necessarily possess unreality or are false; so I have used the words "value-charged story," thereby leaving open the question of reality or unreality, truth or falsity, but indicating that for those who believe them, myths express the most profound meanings of life. This, then, is the justification of my definition of "myth" as a value-charged story expressing to some degree the life orientation of a group and/or individual. I believe that this is a rather commonsense definition and that if strictly adhered to would lead to some measure of clarity.

3. The Relevance of Myth for Religious Discourse

Let us turn now to a consideration of the relevance of myth for religious discourse. Our prior discussion of the meaning of myth already has contained hints that there is a significant relationship between the two. At this point, we will attempt to clarify the nature of that relationship.

The first task in clarifying the relationship between myth and religious discourse is to make as clear as possible what is meant by the words "religious discourse." The capacity for distinguishing religious from non-religious discourse as well as the capacity for distinguishing myth from non-myth is logically prior to the capacity for determining if there is a relationship between the two.

There is, I take it, little difficulty with regard to the word "discourse." The dictionaries I have consulted indicate that the word refers to the formulation and expression of thought in oral or written form. The major difficulty is with the word "religious."

I agree with my colleague, Professor William T. Blackstone, that much of the confusion and ambiguity surrounding the word "religious" can be eliminated if one defines it in terms of its use or function.[6] That is to say, the word "religious" does not refer to some sort of static substantive reality defying changing circumstances in human thought and behavior; rather it is to be understood as referring to certain characteristic roles or functions played by some sentences and beliefs in the discourse and behavior of people. This approach, it seems to me, enables one to formulate a definition which avoids begging-the-question. The definition offered here has been inspired by this approach of Professor Blackstone although the formulation of it which follows is in large part my own. "Religious discourse" comprises the oral or written expression of the beliefs of a group and/or individual concerning the "object (or objects) of devotion"[7] considered to be of greatest value and reality, and in light of which the group and/or individual finds life's most significant purpose and direction in establishing its or his own existence. Notice that this definition does not make an a priori decision as to whether a piece of talk or an object is religious or non-religious. This can be decided only after it has been determined through careful investigation whether or not the piece of talk or the object plays the role designated by the definition. Sentences containing words generally associated with religion like "God," "Christ," or "Covenant" may or may not be religious depending upon whether or not they fulfill the designated role. The works of Biblical scholars, although about the Bible as a religious document, are filled with examples of sentences which are not religious because they do not peform the role designated by the definition.

As Professor Blackstone has indicated, a functional definition like the one just proposed has a number of advantages. (1) "It avoids a narrow, conventional, or provincial view of religion which arbitrarily rules out as religious any beliefs except those of a small specified group."[8] (2) It is not a persuasive definition which restricts discussion to some preconceived area of the "religious." (3) It is impartial "to all religious beliefs in the sense that it is not a reflection of anyone's personal religious views."[9] These comments, I believe, provide a significant justification for the definition.

The restatement of the definitions of "myth" and "religious discourse" should prove instructive here. We have defined "myth" as a value-charged story expressing to some degree the life orientation of a group and/or individual. We have defined religious discourse as the oral or written expression of the beliefs of a group and/or individual concerning the object (or objects) of devotion considered to be of greatest value and reality and in light of which group and/or individual finds life's most significant purpose and direction in establishing its or his own existence. Put into juxtaposition it is apparent that these two definitions have much in common. Both religious discourse and myth are concerned with "value," "reality," and "life orientation" or "establishing existence in terms of purpose and direction." Indeed, they have so much in common that it might seem that we are using two words to designate the same thing. However, this is not the case. A value-charged story need not be concerned with an object of devotion which is considered to be of *greatest* value. An expression of that which is considered to be real, need not be concerned with the *greatest* reality. A story expressing *to some degree* the life orientation of a group and/or individual need not express the *most significant* life purpose and direction of group or individual. It may do all these things, but it need not do them. Myths, then, are often religious, though not always so.

On the other hand, religious discourse as defined is never without some element of myth or the mythical. While it is true that any particular piece of religious discourse may include all types of sentences—descriptive, hortatory, interrogative, tautological—

which in themselves are not mythical but which play a role in expressing a particular religious commitment, no religious discourse can be without the mythical. In terms of our definitions, it would be a logical impossibility for religious discourse to be entirely devoid of the mythical. If it were, it could not be called religious. Of course, a particular piece of religious discourse may not contain myth as a story, but it will contain some mythical elements. That is, it will contain some highly value-charged sentences which had their origin in myths or in beliefs based on myths and, therefore, could be labeled mythical.

Many contemporary theologians are saying that myth or mythical language is essential to religious communication. Perhaps a brief analysis of a few of these positions will help us to understand more fully the relationship of myth and religious language. Unfortunately, our problem is complicated by the fact that "myth" is not always clearly defined nor unambiguously used by the three theologians to be discussed. All three are agreed that myth is of significance for religious discourse, but they are not agreed as to what myth is or as to what its relationship to religious discourse is or should be.

Much of the discussion of myth in contemporary theological circles has been motivated by the writings of the distinguished German theologian and New Testament scholar, Rudolf Bultmann. Bultmann's consideration of myth was motivated by his concern with the problem of communicating the Christian Gospel to contemporary man who is so far removed from the world view of the source of this Gospel, namely, the Bible. In his famous (some would say infamous) essay, "New Testament and Myth,"[10] Bultmann labels the New Testament world outlook as mythical. This includes the New Testament cosmology with its three story universe inhabited by God and his angels and Satan and his demons. It includes evil spirits, miracles, and an apocalyptic eschatology. To the extent that the proclamation of the Christian Gospel is encased in such a mythical view, it is meaningless to contemporary man. Statements in the creeds, for example, presuppose a three story universe and, says Bultmann, "The only honest way of reciting the creeds is to strip the mythological framework from the truth they enshrine."[11]

Throughout this portion of his essay, the discussion seems clear enough provided one accepts Bultmann's sense of the word mythical as referring to a pre-scientific world view. Later, however, Bultmann defines mythology as "the use of imagery to express the other worldly in terms of this world and the divine in terms of human life, the other side in terms of this side."[12] At this point, Bultmann tells us that the task of the theologian and the minister is that of applying the method of demythologizing to the New Testament. In light of his previous discussion, we might assume that Bultmann means by demythologizing the elimination of myth, but he hastens to tell us that such is not the case. Demythologizing is a method of exposition involving interpretation, not elimination of myths.

If the mythology of the New Testament is to be interpreted so that it is intelligible to modern man, it must be done, according to Bultmann, anthropologically or existentially. One must attempt to discover in any myth what the writer is saying about his own existence. Beyond that the question must be asked what meaning this writer's understanding of his own existence might have for man today. The truth of the myth is its existential meaning for modern man. This existential relationship is the decisive thing in every religious expression, and only if it is present is it possible to speak of the truth of a myth. Kendrick Grobel maintains that Bultmann is attempting "to mediate the biblical witness's *intention* by transposing it out of his mythical world of presuppositions into the hearer's non-mythical world of presuppositions in order to reach *his* understanding and will where he is,"[13] and that Bultmann's method of achieving this is to utilize "man's understanding of himself in his world."[14] This is done in terms of Martin Heidegger's philosophy, especially his emphasis on authentic and unauthentic existence, which Bultmann believes to be a secularized reflection of the New Testament view of human life. Questions concerning such aspects of the New Testament faith as the incarnation, the life and teachings of Jesus the Christ, the Cross, and Resurrection become primarily a matter "of self-understanding speaking to self-understanding."[15] Religious statements are to be understood as statements about human existence. To really understand one's own existence is to come to some understanding of being, of the mystery of God, for our existence is incomplete and points beyond itself. This does not mean, however, that the object of faith is entirely subjective. As Bultmann put it, "When we say that faith alone . . . can speak of God, and that therefore when the believer speaks of an act of God he is ipso facto speaking of himself as well, it by no means follows that God has no real existence apart from the believer or the act of believing."[16] It is precisely at this point that Bultmann the theologian is compelled to set the limit of demythologizing for it is difficult, to say the least, to speak of an act of God as an objective reality in existentialist terminology. All that one could do would be to give a phenomenological account of what it means for human beings to live as if there were a God.

There are several difficulties in Bultmann's position regarding the relationship of myth and religious discourse. The word "myth" is used ambiguously. At times he seems to be using the word to designate pre-scientific thought forms or world outlook. At other times, and most certainly in his formal definition as pointed out by Ronald Hepburn,[17] he is using the word in such a loose sense that it would include all pictorial, analogical, and symbolical language. This is certainly confusing for at times it is difficult to determine which sense of "myth" Bultmann means.

Bultmann's formal definition, namely, that "mythology is the use of imagery to express the other worldly in terms of this world and the divine in terms of human life, the other side in terms of this side" is itself confusing. Hepburn remarks that "by his own test itself this definition is partly couched in mythological language."[18] Clearly this is the case and thus there is an element of begging-the-question in this definition.

If Bultmann's use of the words "myth" or "mythical" had been consistent with his formal definition, then as Hepburn has indicated the whole process of demythologizing would have been logically impossible.[19] The definition is wide enough to include analogy. For Bultmann, our talk about God is analogical and thus mythical if the formal definition holds. Therefore, our talk about God cannot be translated into non-mythical statements. But Bultmann does not want to get caught in this trap and so affirms that there is a distinction between mythological and analogical language. Examples of analogies are such expressions as "an act of God," or "the love of God," or "the fatherhood of God." To utter such expressions, says Bultmann, "does not necessarily mean to speak in symbols and imagery. Such speech must be able to convey its full, direct meaning."[20] This statement is odd to say the least. According to John Macquarrie, it most certainly departs from the generally accepted sense of the word "analogical" as referring to indirect talk about God and by implication at least would lead in the direction of a rather crude anthropomorphism which would be abhorrent to Bultmann himself.[21] Thus, Bultmann seems to be caught on the horns of a dilemma. If he remains consistent with his formal definition, demythologizing is logically impossible. If he departs from his formal definition and claims that analogical language is direct talk about God, then he ends in anthropomorphism, for talk of God can be "fully direct," as Macquarrie says, "only if God were precisely like one of ourselves."[22]

It is doubtful that modern man's presuppositions are as non-mythical as Bultmann assumes. If one takes myth simply as a pre-scientific world view, then, of course, modern man's presuppositions are for the most part non-mythical. But as we have seen, there is some justification for the elimination of the pre-scientific world view from the defining characteristics of "myth." In our view, a myth is not a myth simply because it is a false story. Any responsible person would agree with Bultmann that primitive thought forms must be eliminated or radically reinterpreted if the Christian gospel is to make sense to modern man. But it is highly doubtful that a translation into a language which in all respects is subject to human truth-criteria can ever be made. If we understand myth as a value-charged story expressing to some degree the life orientation of a group and/or individual, then the very presuppositions of our truth-criteria are themselves mythical. Thus, we can say that the problem for theologians today is not demythologizing but remythologizing. That is to say, the primitive, pre-scientific elements which accompany ancient myths will be eliminated, morally offensive elements will be removed or shown to illustrate themes which are not in themselves morally objectionable, and those myth themes which provide some sense and direction for life even though they transcend truth-criteria will be preserved and made meaningful to contemporary man through such expositions as are needed. But it is logically impossible for these expositions to be free of some degree of mythical language.

Another interesting theological position concerning myth is

that of Paul Tillich. For Tillich, myth is much more than a primitive world view. Rather, it is "a whole of symbols, expressing man's relation to that which concerns him ultimately, the ground and meaning of his life."[23] There is no such thing as an unmythical attitude, for myth is essential to human life and thought. Even science, when it uses concepts that are transcendent to observable, factual reality, comes into a new mythical situation and becomes myth-creative. Thus, myth or the mythical, whether expressed in science or in religion, is an element in life that cannot be eliminated. Myths cannot be removed from man's spiritual life. They are present in every act of faith, for faith could have no language without symbol and myth. We cannot eliminate myth without eliminating faith.[24]

For Tillich, myths operate in a realm other than that of literal descriptive discourse which is verifiable or falsifiable by existing scientific truth tests. There is no conflict between these two realms if myths are not taken literally. Thus, he speaks of "broken myths"[25] and of "deliteralization."[26] This latter term he prefers to Bultmann's "demythologization" for he finds a serious ambiguity in the discussion of demythologization due to the failure to distinguish two meanings in the use of the term. Demythologization can mean the attempt to free Christian theology from a literalistic view of myth, and Tillich agrees that this is a necessary task. But demythologization can also mean the elimination of myths in the attempt to express religious belief in the language of science and morals. This attempt must be rejected because, Tillich affirms, "it would deprive religion of its language."[27]

Although Tillich affirms that myths are essential for religious language and that our task is one of deliteralizing rather than demythologizing, it can be questioned just how much he escapes demythologizing when it comes to his actual treatment of some of the biblical myths. When Tillich speaks of the Genesis myth of the Fall as symbolizing a transcendent fall, a "transition from essence to existence"[28] in the universal human situation, has he not ceased deliteralizing and begun to demythologize? Even Tillich himself admits that this is a "half-way demythologizing."[29] It is only "half-way" because, Tillich claims, the words "transition from essence to existence" contain a temporal element, and to speak of the divine in temporal terms is to speak mythologically.

It is also a "half-way demythologizing" to define the "New

Being," which appears in Jesus as the Christ, as Tillich does. He says, "New Being is essential being under the conditions of existence, conquering the gap between essence and existence."[30] Since for Tillich the only non-mythical statement that can be made about the divine is that God is Being-itself, there is still, in view of its temporal element, some myth remaining in this Christological sentence. Much of it, however, has been eliminated in this highly ontological reconstruction.

In contrast to Bultmann who asserts that we ought to translate the Christian myths into literally true statements, Tillich claims that we cannot do so without "depriving religion of its language." Yet, in the actual exposition of the Christian myths, he proceeds to do just that. In their actual exposition both Bultmann and Tillich eliminate myths even though they may claim to be simply "reinterpreting" or "deliteralizing." Bultmann does so in favor of an existentialist ethical interpretation and Tillich in favor of an existentialist ontological interpretation. It is in their philosophies that their actual disagreement is to be found, for in contrast to Bultmann, Tillich believes that Christian doctrine has an ontological sense as well as an existentialist sense.

I think it is fair to say that Tillich's discussion of myth avoids much of the ambiguity found in Bultmann's. His definition avoids taking myth as a false story. One might raise a question with regard to his affirmation that myth expresses "man's relation to that which concerns him ultimately," namely, doesn't this restrict too narrowly the denotation of the word? Value-charged stories we would want to call myths certainly express the concerns of men but they need not be ultimate concerns. Of course, Tillich is primarily interested in religious myths and here the concerns expressed would be ultimate.

There is another and more serious difficulty with Tillich's position. He claims that the only non-mythical thing that can be said about God is that God is being itself. Everything that is participates in the power of being including myths and symbols. Myths and symbols cannot be criticized in terms of anything other than myths and symbols and yet some express more adequately than others ultimate concern or being itself. But if all symbols and myths participate in the power of being, how can one distinguish between adequate and inadequate myths? Apparently, Tillich would answer that those myths are adequate which serve as a means by which one is grasped by the power of being and which do not usurp the place of being itself. Is this not to make the criterion for adequate myths one's own intuition or feelings? As William P. Alston has pointed out, "There is no reason to suppose that [psychologically] ultimate concern must be directed to what is [ontologically] ultimate."[31]

A third theologian who has made much use of the word "myth" in his writing is Reinhold Niebuhr. For Niehubr, myth is much more than a fanciful or false story preserved from ancient times; rather it is a way of talking about certain aspects of reality which cannot be stated in terms of empirically verifiable propositions. Such aspects of reality include value, beauty, and religion. A religious myth is one which "seeks to comprehend facts and occurrences in terms of their organic relation to the whole conceived in teleological terms."[32] It is the means whereby the supra-rational invades the rational, and the supra-historical the historical. Transposing Santayana's sentence that "Poetry is religion which is no longer believed," Niebuhr affirms that "Religion is poetry which is believed."[33] Myth, then, is indispensable for religious discourse, for in religion what can be said literally is of little significance.

Thus, Niebuhr agrees with Tillich in rejecting Bultmann's program of demythologizing. He feels that this program has distorted the purity of the Christian Gospel due in part to its confusion of "prescientific myths" with "permanent myths"[34] and in part to the inadequacy of existentialist philosophy to serve as a medium of communicating the Christian message. In the first case, demythologizing too often throws out the baby with the dirty bath water. In the second case, existentialism, while appreciating the freedom of man, does not understand the profundity of the biblical concept of sin. We must, of course, eliminate pre-scientific myths, but we should retain permanent myths, for any attempt to reinterpret them in terms of philosophical or scientific concepts leads to a distortion of the meaning we need to provide direction and significance for our lives.

It is this conviction which leads Niebuhr to reject Tillich's attempt to provide an ontological basis in terms of which the Christian message is to be communicated. Metaphysics of any kind is likely to overemphasize some one aspect of reality to the exclusion of others and thus to present too simple and one-sided an interpretation of reality including human existence. Tillich's ontology such as is demonstrated in his discussion of the myth of the Fall and Christ as the New Being is no exception. Concerning it Niebuhr says, "I do not believe that ontological categories can do justice to the freedom either of the divine or of the human person, or to the unity of the person in his involvement in and transcendence over the temporal flux or that the sin of man and the forgiveness by God of man's sin or the dramatic variety of man's history can be comprehended in ontological categories."[35] To try to translate the Christian message into ontological language is to end in changing the very nature of the Christian faith itself. The "permanent myths" must be retained. These myths, such as the creation, the fall, the incarnation, the atonement, the resurrection, are the enduring expressions and creators of faith. They are capable of continued reinterpretation, yet remain when the reinterpretation is found not to be final.

For Niebuhr, myths arise in man's experience due to his attempt to speak of transcendent realities, of that odd combination of mystery and meaning with which life confronts man, and they are verified in two ways, a negative and a positive. The negative way is to show that other ways (especially metaphysical) "of explaining or dissolving the mystery and meaning which governs and surrounds us leads to observable miscalculations in regard to the nature of man and history."[36] The positive way is through a certain type of experience, namely, that type which is found in the area of history and freedom transcending the scientific realm of strict measurement and control. Religious myths are verifiable in this realm. "That 'God was in Christ reconciling the world unto Himself' is verifiable," says Niebuhr, "in the experience of everyone who experiences the mercy and new life which flows from true repentance in the encounter with God."[37]

While Niebuhr has avoided some of the pitfalls in the positions of Bultmann and Tillich, there are still some difficulties in his own position.

1. In his definitions of "myth" as the expression of transcendent realities and of "religion" as poetry we believe, Niebuhr seems to imply that all religious discourse is mythical. We have seen that for any particular piece of discourse to be labeled "religious" some mythical sentences are necessary but that given a functional definition of "religious" some sentences in

this discourse may be descriptive, hortatory, interrogative, and tautological. The entire discourse, inclusive of all these types of sentences, is called "religious" because it serves to express the beliefs of an individual or group concerning the object of devotion considered to be of greatest value and reality, and in light of which one's existence is established. Further, Niebuhr's definition of myth as the expression of transcendent realities seems to imply the actual objective existence of these realities apart from the convictions of the believer. They may in fact so exist, but should not the *definition* leave this as an open question? The definition of myth as a value-charged story expressing to some degree the life orientation of a group and/or individual does not imply a pre-judgment as to whether the realities expressed in these stories do or do not exist apart from the convictions of the believers.

2. While Niebuhr clearly rejects the popular understanding of "myth" as a fanciful story, he does not do so consistently. As we have seen, he speaks of "pre-scientific myths." Is this not to use "myth" in its popular sense? Would not greater clarity have been achieved by dropping the word "myth" here and replacing it by the words "world view" or "primitive science?" Is it not the case that many (perhaps most) of the myths we accept are prescientific in the sense that they had their origins in periods prior to the advent of modern science? Is it not also the case that we need not reject an entire myth as expressive of cherished convictions in our life orientation even though it contains some primitive science, cosmology, or world view as accompanying characteristics which cannot be accepted as factually true?

3. Perhaps a more serious difficulty in Niebuhr's position is to be found in his affirmation that "permanent myths" are verified in human experience. The difficulty centers around his use of the word "verified." I strongly suspect that the use of this word was due, at least in part, to its honorific status in ordinary usage arising from its association with the sciences. If the word is taken in the sense that it has in philosophy and the sciences, then it can be demonstrated that Niebuhr's claim cannot be established. In these fields a proposition expressed by a sentence is verified if it is possible to secure publicly observable evidence that the state-of-affairs labeled by the sentence is in fact the case. The proposition expressed by the sentence, "It is raining," can be

verified or falsified because it is possible to secure enough publicly observable evidence to make it highly probable that such a state-of-affairs either is or is not the case. Is it possible to apply this sense of verification to Niebuhr's "permanent myths"? I think not. Consider Niebuhr's example of a "permanent myth" that is verifiable in human experience, namely, "God was in Christ reconciling the world unto Himself." Does this sentence express a proposition concerning which it is possible to secure some agreed upon publicly observable evidence? Would the believer permit anything to count against the truth he finds in this sentence; and if he would not permit anything to count against it, can the sentence be said to have empirical meaning; and if it does not have empirical meaning, can it be verified? It cannot, if we take the word "verification" and its cognates in what we might call the strong sense which we have just described.

Obviously, Niebuhr does not use the word in this strong sense since he affirms that myths are not empirically verifiable but may be verified on their own level. What he seems to mean by this is something akin to pragmatic justification. That is, our belief in permanent myths is justified due to the practical consequences which such a belief has in our lives. It seems to me that Niebuhr's discussion would have been clearer had he used a term such as pragmatic justification rather than verification.

Earlier in our discussion we argued that myth was essential for religious discourse. As we have seen, two of the three theologians considered, Tillich and Niebuhr, support this claim although there are considerable differences between the two and between their positions and the one presented here. If myths are essential for religious discourse and belief, how are we to judge which ones to accept?

Throughout this discussion it has been emphasized that given our definition of myth as a value-charged story expressing to some degree the life orientation of a group and/or individual, myth is not just a fanciful or false story or belief. If we attempt to falsify myths, we may find some that can be shown to be false in whole or in part; others we will find impossible to falsify either logically or empirically or practically. It is not their myth character which makes them false. As we have seen, Bultmann apparently fails to recognize this since he would have us eliminate certain myths and retain others only so long as they are capable of existentialist reinterpretation. Tillich and Niebuhr do recognize this point although Tillich is not entirely consistent here since he proceeds to provide some myths with an ontological reinterpretation. Niebuhr remains consistent on this point since he rejects existentialist and ontological reinterpretations and eliminates only those myths or portions of myths which can be falsified. I would agree with Niebuhr here. No myth or portion of a myth which is demonstrated to be false can be accepted any more than anything else which is falsified. However, the theme expressed, the understanding of the life orientation, in the false myth may transcend falsifiability and thus be expressed in a different mythical language which is not falsified or falsifiable.

What of myths which transcend the practical, empirical, or logical possibility of verification? Are there criteria which may guide one in deciding which myths to accept? Tillich's talk of the myth grasping one leads ultimately, so it seems to me, to an appeal to some form of mystical intuition which is entirely too subjective and arbitrary. If I have interpreted him correctly, Niebuhr appeals to a pragmatic justification and this, I think, is a much more adequate criterion.

To Niebuhr's I would add three other closely related criteria and the four together would, I believe, provide a much more self-conscious and rigorous basis upon which one might choose the religious myths which will serve to express the object of devotion which he takes to be of greatest value and reality and in terms of which he establishes his existence. These criteria are as follows. (1) One might apply the test of internal consistency. Great care should be exercised here. Myths often express paradoxes which upon first glance appear self-contradictory but which upon more careful scrutiny and seen in a larger context are not self-contradictory at all. For example, Jesus' paradox "For whoever would save his life will lose it, and whoever loses his life for my sake will find it" (Matthew 16:25) appears self-contradictory as it stands, but seen in the larger context of his teachings it is not self-contradictory. However, that which is expressed in an actual self-contradictory assertion cannot possibly be the case and how can that which cannot possibly be the case become an item of faith? (2) A second criterion that could be used is to achieve as great a degree of coherence as possible between the myths which one accepts. For example, it certainly would make no sense to accept the biblical myths of the one God and at the same time to accept the Greek polytheistic myths. (3) A third criterion that could be applied is that of comprehensiveness. That is to say, a body of myths would be judged as adequate not only because each one of the body was internally consistent and there was coherence between the myths in this group, but also because these myths were more inclusive in perspective and universal in scope. For example, myths of a God who was concerned about all men would be deemed more adequate than myths concerning a God who was concerned only about the members of a particular ethnic or national group. (4) To these three will be added the fourth, namely, pragmatic justification. This involves the ability of the myths to keep men going against defeat, frustration, disappointment, to motivate men to resist those forces which feed on hatred and enjoy the sufferings of others, to serve as a preservative and detergent for institutions and institutional processes and to provide some sense of timeless dignity and worth for human life.

To defend myth in terms of Tertullian's rule, "I believe because it is absurd," is not a real option for many and perhaps the majority of people today. The criteria I have proposed will not enable us to say that the religious myths we believe are true in the sense that they are empirically verified, but if rigorously applied these criteria will permit us to hold to and express our religious convictions without falling into the pit of absurdity.

Notes

1. Webster's *Third New International Dictionary* (Springfield: G & C Merriam Company, 1963).

2. Mircea Eliade, *Myths, Dreams and Mysteries* (New York: Harper and Brothers, 1960); *The Myth of the Eternal Return* (New York: Pantheon Books, 1954); G. van der Leeuw, *Religion in Essence and Manifestation* (London: George Allen and Unwin, 1938); Willem F. Zuurdeeg, *An Analytical Philosophy of Religion* (New York: Abingdon Press, 1958). In Chapter v, Professor Zuurdeeg summarized the findings of two Dutch scholars, W. B. Kristensen and K. A. H. Hedding. All of these scholars have emphasized what might be called the "participating" feature of myth.

3. Mircea Eliade, *Myths, Dreams and Mysteries*, pp. 15, 24.

4. Thomas J. J. Altizer, "The Religious Meaning of Myth and Symbol," *Truth, Myth and Symbol*, eds. Altizer, Beardslee, Young (Englewood Cliffs: Prentice-Hall, 1962), p. 93.

5. Willem F. Zuurdeeg, *An Analytical Philosophy of Religion*, p. 174.

6. William T. Blackstone, *The Problem of Religious Knowledge* (Englewood Cliffs: Prentice-Hall, 1963), pp. 36–46.

7. Ibid., p. 39.

8. Ibid., p. 41.

9. Ibid., p. 45.

10. *Kerygma and Myth*, ed. Hans Werner Bartsch (London: S. P. C. K., 1953), pp. 1–44.

11. Ibid., p. 4.

12. Ibid., p. 10, n. 2.

13. "Bultmann's Problem of New Testament 'Mythology,'" *Journal of Biblical Literature* 70 (June 1951): 100.

14. Ibid.

15. Ibid.

16. *Kerygma and Myth*, p. 199.

17. "Demythologizing and the Problem of Validity," *New Essays in Philosophical Theology*, eds. Flew and MacIntyre (New York: The Macmillan Company, 1955), p. 229.

18. Ibid.

19. Ibid.

20. Rudolf Bultmann, *Jesus Christ and Mythology* (New York: Charles Scribner's Sons, 1958), p. 68.

21. John Macquarrie, *The Scope of Demythologizing* (New York: Harper and Brothers, 1960), p. 205, n. 1.

22. Ibid.

23. "The Present Theological Situation in Light of the Continental European Development," *Theology Today* 6 (October 1949): 306.

24. "The Religious Symbol," *The Journal of Liberal Religion* 2 (Summer 1940): 23–24. Also *The Dynamics of Faith* (New York: Harper and Brothers, 1957), pp. 49–50.

25. *Dynamics of Faith*, pp. 48–54.

26. *Systematic Theology*, 2 (Chicago: University of Chicago Press, 1957), p. 15.

27. Ibid., p. 152.

28. Ibid., p. 29.

29. Ibid.

30. Ibid., pp. 118–119.

31. "Tillich's Conception of a Religious Symbol," *Religious Experience and Truth*, ed. Sidney Hook (New York: New York University Press, 1961), p. 21.

32. "The Truth in Myths," *The Nature of Religious Experience*, eds. Bixler, Calhoun, Niebuhr (New York: Harper and Brothers, 1937), p. 119.

33. Ibid. Similar discussions of myth are to be found in *An Interpretation of Christian Ethics* (New York: Meridian Books, 1956), pp. 20–21, and *Beyond Tragedy* (New York: Scribner's, 1937), pp. 3–24.

34. *The Self and the Dramas of History* (New York: Scribner's, 1955), p. 97.

35. "Reply to Interpretation and Criticism," *Reinhold Niebuhr, His Religious, Social, and Political Thought*, eds. Kegley and Bretall (New York: The Macmillan Company, 1956), p. 433.

36. *The Self and the Dramas of History*, p. 98.

37. Ibid.

AN INQUIRY INTO THE MEANING OF NEGATION IN THE DIALECTICAL LOGICS OF EAST AND WEST

Thomas J. J. Altizer

The theologian cannot but have grave misgivings in beholding the contemporary spectacle of the philosophical quest for meaning in religious language. One almost suspects that the analytic philosopher is persuaded that only common language is meaningful, an attitude which reduces religious language to the level of popular piety. Not only does the philosopher—here following an ancient Western tradition—refuse to acknowledge the existence of a language which is intrinsically religious, but he also insists upon approaching the problem of religious language from the point of view of the dominant tradition of Western logic, a logic grounded in the laws of identity and the excluded middle, which is to say a logic whose most basic postulate is the denial of contradiction. Now it is a simple fact that all authentic forms of religious language, that is, all language which is the product of a uniquely religious vision, are grounded by one means or another in a dialectical logic, that is, in a mode of understanding which assumes the *necessity* of contradiction. Such must inevitably be the case if only because all authentic forms of religion are directed against the given, against the world, or, we might more accurately say, against the "positive." Faith, in all its forms, is the product of negation. Yet this negation is but the other side of the deepest affirmation. Only with the disappearance, the reversal, or the transformation of reality, of the "positive," does the religious Reality appear. Therefore the dialectical coincidence of negation and affirmation is the innermost reality of the life of faith, and all forms of religion which have assumed a fully philosophical form have either adopted or created a dialectical logic. Indeed, dialectical thinking has always dominated the Orient, but in the Occident, while briefly appearing in Heraclitus, it was overthrown by the rise to power of the Platonic and Aristotelian schools, only to reappear sporadically and in a subterranean way in various forms of mysticism. Perhaps the medieval Cabala is the purest expression of dialectical thinking in the West; but by the seventeenth century, despite the dialectical form of Eckhart's mystical theology and the efforts of Nicolas Cusanus, it had become necessary to re-discover a dialectical method of thought, a re-discovery effected by the simple German cobbler, Jacob Boehme, and a re-discovery which made possible Hegel's logic, the only fully dialectical logic which the West has ever produced.

Negation is the most important mode or movement of dialectical logic, and in this paper I will examine the meaning of negation in Buddhist logic, by general agreement the greatest logical system evolved in India, with the purpose of comparing this Indian understanding of negation with the meaning of negation in Hegel's logic. And so formulated, it becomes clear that the real goal is to inquire into the relation between the dialectical thinking of East and West, a goal that in this case will be sought by way of a concentration upon the religious grounds of these respective logics. Let me also confess that this will not be a scholarly paper: I shall simply limit myself to Th. Stcherbatsky's great work on Buddhist logic (it might be noted that this is the only book-length study of the subject in print, and that the second volume of this work contains translations of significant Sanskrit and Tibetan texts), and then to Hegel's *Science of Logic*, ignoring the various commentaries which his logic has elicited. Hopefully such rashness will be tolerated in one who is neither a philosopher nor an historian, and who undertakes this task with the conviction that he is therein engaged in a theological quest.

Before approaching the actual system of Buddhist logic, it is necessary to speak briefly about its mystical ground. This ground lies in the Mahayana Buddhist category of *sunya*, which in one way or another is the foundation of all the later forms of Buddhism. At about the time of the beginning of the Christian era, the Madhyamika school of Mahayana Buddhism arose with its insistence upon the ultimate oneness of reality, its denial that causal, conceptual, or differentiated thought can grasp the real, and its paradoxical identification of nirvana (the radical sacred) and *samsara* (the radical profane). Here, the mystical Reality known to the Buddhist seer demands that the reality known in cognitive thought and common experience be thrust into an absolute Nothing or Void (*sunyata*). But to the Madhyamika Buddhist, the voidness of "reality" (*samsara*) is simply the hither side of ultimate Reality (nirvana) itself: when known through consciousness and craving (*tanha*), reality appears as *samsara*; but when known through mystical intuition (*prajna*) and self-giving compassion (*karuna*), reality appears as nirvana. In *The Conception of Buddhist Nirvana*—which along with T. R. V. Murti's *The Central Conception of Buddhism* is one of the two most enlightening books on the Madhyamika school—Stcherbatsky describes this Mahayana position as follows:

> In Mahayana all parts or elements are unreal (*sunya*), and only the whole, i.e., the Whole of the wholes, is real. The definition of reality (*tattva*) in Mahayana is the following one: "uncognizable from without, quiescent, undifferentiated in words, unrealisable in concepts, non-plural—this is the essence of reality." . . . Since we use the term "relative" to describe the fact that a thing can be identified only by mentioning its relations to something else, and becomes meaningless without these relations, implying at the same time that the thing in question is unreal, we safely, for want of a better solution, can translate the word *sunya* by relative or contingent, and the term *sunyata* by relativity or contingency. This is in any case better than to translate it by "void" which signification the term has in common life, but not as a technical term in philosophy. That the term *sunya* is in Mahayana a synonym of dependent existence and means not something void, but something "devoid" of independent reality, with the implication that nothing short of the whole possesses independent reality, and with the further implication that the whole forbids every formulation by concept or speech, since they can only bifurcate reality and never directly seize it—this is attested by an overwhelming mass of evidence in all the Mahayana literature.[1]

Let it also be noted that the Madhyamika school knew both a negative and a positive dialectic, the negative being directed to the dissolution of all concepts so as to make possible a positive dialectical affirmation of the ultimately Real. Again, these positive and negative poles of the dialectic must be held in even balance, for the intuitive vision of the saint is impossible apart from the continuous negation of the thought world of the mind.

The Madhyamika school effected a virtual condemnation of logic, but by the fifth century A.D., particularly through the work of the brothers Asanga and Vasubandhu, a new interest in logic arose in Buddhism, which within five hundred years became so overwhelming as to supersede all of the former theoretical expressions of Buddhism in India. The great names in Buddhist logic are Dignaga, Dharmakirti, and Dharmottara, who were followed by various schools of commentators, first in India and then in Tibet, where Buddhist logic has remained alive until the present day. By intention, Buddhist logic has no special relation with Buddhism as a religion, it simply claims to be the natural and general logic of the human understanding. However, as Stcherbatsky says, it also claims to be critical:

> Entities whose existence is not sufficiently warranted by the laws of logic are mercilessly repudiated, and in this point Buddhist logic only keeps faithful to the ideas with which Buddhism started. It then denied a God, it denied the Soul, it denied Eternity. It admitted nothing but the transient flow of evanescent events and their final eternal quiescence in *nirvana*. Reality, according to Buddhists, is kinetic, not static, but logic, on the other hand, imagines a reality stabilized in concepts and names. The ultimate aim of Buddhist logic is to explain the relation between a moving reality and the static constructions of thought.[2]

All Buddhists are radical nominalists, insisting that the dichotomizing activity of the mind wholly alienates its conceptual products from the concrete contingency of real events. Moreover Buddhist nominalists are more radical than their European counterparts; here the particular apprehended in sensation (as opposed to perception) is the bare particular, containing nothing whatsoever of the universal qualities that are a product of the conceptual process. Consequently Buddhist logic assumes a sharp epistemological distinction between the senses and the intellect as two different instruments of cognition.[3] This transcendental difference between sensibility and understanding is in fact the ultimate ground of its system,[4] and the Buddhist drama of cognition finally has but two characters: "Reality" and "Ideality," the flow of radically contingent events and the static imaginative constructions of the mind.[5]

Despite the claims of Buddhist logic to be the simple laws of the human understanding and the pragmatic instrument which leads to successful action, it is all too clearly grounded in the earlier Hinayana conception of the *dharmas* as the ultimately real events and in the Mahayana mystical category of *sunyata*. An ultimately real event (*dharma*) can only be cognized in pure sensation, in a sensation which is purely passive and which is therefore wholly opposed to the spontaneous activity of the intellect. Such an event is unique, it is absolutely dissimilar to every other event, it has no extension in space and no duration in time, thus Stcherbatsky calls it the "point-instant" (*ksana*) of reality.[6] Such a point-instant is "pure existence," it is indivisible, is pure efficiency; and thus it is transcendental, for it is both non-empirical and unutterable. Nevertheless, the point-instant is real, it is even reality itself, and an object which is not connected with a sensation, with sensible reality, is either pure imagination or a mere name. The consequence of this position is that all super-sensuous objects are uncognizable, and hence metaphysical knowledge becomes impossible. Furthermore, the objects of our language and concepts are pure imagination, mere words, they are wholly alienated from reality.[7] No definition of a thing is possible, we can only know its relations, and the definiteness of an object or thing as known in our intellect must be in inverse ratio to the vividness of its presence in our perception.[8] But pure sensation and the corresponding pure object are not truly distinct: "They are one Ultimate Reality dichotomized into Subject and Object by that same faculty of constructive imagination which is the architect of the whole empirical world and which always works by the dichotomizing or dialectical method."[9] In other words, sensation and understanding are the products of the differentiated or fallen state of our mind and experience, and, as we shall see, these modes of cognition disappear in the mystical vision of the saint.

The Buddhist logician's epistemology is built upon the foundation of a difference in principle between a direct and an indirect knowledge, between immediate sensation and the inferential process of conception. Pure sensation indicates the presence of a thing or an event, its mere presence and nothing more. It is followed by the construction of an image of the event, for perception is sensation followed by conception. The act of conception is fundamentally an act of judgment:

> "What is a judgment?" asks a Buddhist in the course of a discussion regarding the reality of the external world. That is to say, what is the volitional act by which I decide that an image must be identified with a point-instant of external reality? He answers, "to judge means to conceive." Both inference and sense-perception contain judgments, but an inference deals with conceptions (directly), it is "in its essence an act of conceiving," whereas perception, or a perceptual judgment, is an act of conceiving (indirectly), because it is a sensation which "calls forth a conception." Now, if a judgment, besides being a judgment, i.e., a decision, is also an act of conceiving, what does the term "conception" properly mean? The answer is that to conceive means to imagine, or to construct an object in imagination. The object conceived is an object imagined. To imagine productively means to produce unity in difference, to synthesize in a (fictitious) unity a variety of time, place and condition. The expression of this synthesis is the judgment of the form "this is that," in which the non-synthetic element "thisness" is coupled with the synthetic element of "thatness."[10]

Accordingly, there is no real difference between a perceptual judgment and a conception, or between a concept and an image. All images and concepts are a product of our "productive imagination." "Judgment," says Dharmottara, "means to deal with one's own internal reflex, which is not an external object, in the conviction that it is an external object."[11] Thus judgment is an illusive objectification of the image necessitated by an intrinsic necessity of our understanding to project an internal image into the external world.

Although Stcherbatsky is silent on this subject, we need not hesitate to say that this logical theory of perception and judgment is a positive development of the negative dialectic of the Madhyamika school. Moreover, the real heart of Buddhist logic, its theory of negation, obviously has a mystical ground. Negation is always the work of the understanding, interpreting a given sensation on its negative side, through the action of memory. Thus, negation in this sense (*apoha*) is the negative perception of a present thing; as Stcherbatsky remarks, here, the *presence* is absent, but the perception of an absent thing is present in the imagination.[12] However, a negation is implied in every affirmative proposition, and therefore every proposition is a negative proposition. This fact creates what the Buddhists understand as the dialectical ground of all thought, for thought itself is created by negation in the sense of opposition (*virodha*).

"How is it," asks Dharmottara, "that the same cognition includes a part which is being determined and a part which is its determination?" "Is it not a contradiction to assume in the same unit a cause and its own effect?" And he answers: this is possible—by Negation! Indeed a pure sensation produced by a patch of blue receives definiteness by a negation of the non-blue, i.e., the Understanding interprets an indefinite sensation as being a definite image of the blue by contrasting it with non-blue. The same thing differently regarded becomes as though it were different itself. The objectivity is founded on causality *plus* identity. Thus it is that direct and indubitable cognition is only pure sensation. It contains every-thing. It is the richest in contents and the poorest in thought. But thought makes it definite by negation. Negation is the essence of thought. Definiteness, understanding, conformity, "formity," negation, repudiation of the contrary, image, concept, dichotomy, are but different manners of developing the one fundamental act of pure sensation. The Thing as it is in itself is disclosed by representing it as it is in its non-self, "in the other."[13]

And, as Stcherbatsky observes, this Buddhist understanding of negation as the essence of thought has its Western counterpart only in Hegel.

In Buddhist logic, judgment, as well as all conception, is rooted in contradiction, a contradiction deriving from the dichotomizing activity of the mind, an activity which creates an artificial separation both between subject and object and between one class of objects and another. All active thought is dichotomous, as is every act of consciousness, except its purely passive part, the pure sensation. The Buddhist law of contradiction is simply the expression of the fact that all cognition is dichotomizing and relative: "We can actively cognize or determine a thing only by opposing it to what it is not."[14] What we know as the object, an object identical with itself, is in fact an imaginative construction of our mind. There are no identical real things, every thing or event is radically particular, radically unique, for every variation in time and space makes the thing "another" thing. Therefore things, events, or objects are similar or identical only insofar as our minds do not discern their differences or their "otherness." Only by a negation of the concrete contingency of a thing or an event can we know or experience the event as an object. Accordingly, as Stcherbatsky notes, what we know as the object is wholly the product of the negative or negating activity of the cognitive process:

> If A is related to a non-A just as in the same way in which a non-A is related to A, it is clear that the negation of a non-A will be equal to A. If there is in the blue nothing more than its opposition to the non-blue, it is clear that the opposition to the non-blue will be nothing else than the blue itself. Since all things are relative, every thing, except the ultimate reality of the point-instant, is nothing but the counterpart of its own negation.[15]

Consequently, the difference or opposition between the objects of our understanding is "logical" and not "real," it is constructed by the understanding, and thus is a product of "contradiction," of the dichotomizing activity of the mind.

If the theory of negation is the cornerstone of Buddhist logic, it must also be apparent that Buddhist logic is ultimately grounded in the negation of thought, and this ultimate negation can only have a religious or mystical ground. A contemporary American philosopher, Karl H. Potter, has clearly and decisively formulated this truth:

> Reality, then, is a steady stream of point-instants of energy, momentary forceful occurrences which "do something," which are constantly correlated with others in recurrent patterns. In addition to their function as occasions for later events in those patterns, though, they also, through the dependence-relation of similarity, cause a phenomenon known as conceptualization, involving a differentiation of a concept into two polar notions, the "I" and the "that." Concepts are unreal, since they don't

do anything. They are erroneous, for they clothe the uncharacterized point-instants of energy with attributes which are distinguished for the satisfaction of the erroneously distinguished "I." All conceptualization, therefore, is erroneous for the Buddhist logician, and conceptualization is the necessary condition for bondage which can be broken to obtain freedom. To gain freedom, we must train ourselves not to think of an "I" distinct from a "that," and to do that, we must train ourselves not to think of "thats" clothed in different attributes. By doing this, we gain freedom; we also gain a direct insight into the things-in-themselves which constitute the stream of reality. Science, therefore, properly understood, constitutes the path towards salvation. . . .[16]

Buddhist logic calls us to an understanding of our thought processes as a means of liberating us from these processes, as a means of dissolving the speaker and the thinker, the "I" and the mind, with the conviction that it is precisely this dissolution or negation which is the way to freedom or salvation.

It is essential to all schools of Buddhist thought, including Buddhist logic, to maintain that the Buddha and all "metaphysical objects" lie beyond all possible experience and are absolutely unknowable to the cognitive processes of the mind. The Buddha and nirvana itself transcend time and space, and we can neither think nor speak anything about them whatsoever. Nevertheless, in the Mahayana schools, nirvana is reality itself; and it becomes wholly present through "direct experience," an experience that is impossible for consciousness, if only because, as Dharmakirti says: "Every consciousness and every mental phenomenon are self-conscious."[17] Direct experience is present only in the intuition of the Buddhist saint, an intuition that is only possible through the total dissolution of the self. Dharmottara, in commenting upon Dharmakirti's definition of the intuition of the saint as deep meditation on "transcendental reality," says:

It has indeed the vividness (of direct perception), and just for this reason it (ceases to be) a construction. Constructed (synthetic) knowledge would apprehend the (same) reality in mental images capable of coalescing with words, (indirectly including) experiences (which go back to the time) of the formation of language. . . . This (synthetic knowledge) apprehends something that does not really exist, and since it does not apprehend its object as something present before the observer, it lacks the vividness (of direct perception) without which it remains a construction. But when this vividness is reached it becomes non-constructed (direct, non-synthetic knowledge). Moreover it is not contradicted by experience, since (the object of meditation) which is being apprehended represents the "pure" object (the point-instants of efficiency that are elicited) by logical (analysis). Hence it is direct knowledge, just as (sensation) and other varieties of direct cognition are. Yoga is ecstatic (direct) contemplation. The man who possesses this faculty is a saint.[18]

In other words, through direct or immediate experience, subject and object coalesce, the knowing or the active subject, a subject created by self-consciousness, disappears, and the object appears no longer as "object," but as ultimate Reality itself. This means that the unknowable point-instant or thing-in-itself, which Buddhist logic postulates as the ultimate cause of cognition, is, from the transcendental point of view of mystical intuition, the final Absolute. As one of the Buddhist commentators, Jinendrabuddhi, says: "From the standpoint of 'Thisness' (i.e., the absolute Reality or the Thing-in-Itself), there is no difference at all (between subject and object), but hampered as we are by Transcendental Illusion, all that we know is exclusively its indirect appearance as differentiated by the construction of subject and object."[19]

Now, in Buddhist logic, "pure existence" or the point-instant is never a predicate, but is always the ultimate subject of every judgment and inference.[20] But if it is the subject of every inference, it is a subject which is artificially differentiated or dichotomized by the imaginative or constructive activity of the mind. Thus this very subject when known directly or immediately manifests itself as the final Absolute, personified as the Buddha in his Cosmic Body. Finally, it is this very Absolute which is negated by the differentiating activity of mind and experience, and when this negation is in turn negated by the direct experience of selfless meditation, then the Absolute is truly known in its identification with all reality (nirvana is *samsara*). Thought is therefore the deepest obstacle to release, the greatest barrier to freedom; but by identifying thought with the activity of negation the Buddhist system of logic could abolish the positive ground of thought and thereby make possible its dissolution. Indeed, when thought is fully understood as negation, it ceases to be real, its world becomes illusion, and it reveals itself as being the hither side of absolute freedom and release.

Stcherbatsky maintains that the Buddhist understanding of thought as negation is identical with Hegel's understanding of thought; but whereas Hegel reaches the voidness of the Absolute through logic, Buddhism does so only through "translogic," for Buddhism knows the "body" of the world, a "body" which in no sense shares the negativity of the "soul."[21] The Buddhist knows this trans-metaphysical "body" both *by* affirmation and *as* affirmation, hence he is closed to the more radical negativity of Hegel's metaphysical logic, where reality is known in its ultimate form *by* and *as* negativity. Before examining the meaning and the validity of this claim, we must first examine the meaning of negation in Hegel's thought. Already, in his early theological writings, while discussing the meaning of sacrifice in worship, Hegel remarks that this "aimless destruction for destruction's sake . . . proves to be the only religious relation to absolute objects."[22] This conviction remained central in Hegel's thought, and when we learn, as many scholars tell us, that negation is the one specific and unique element in Hegel's dialectic, we may ask whether Hegel's dialectical understanding of negation does not finally have a Christian ground. In the famous preface to *The Phenomenology of Mind*, immediately after having declared that everything depends upon grasping and expressing the ultimate truth not as "Substance" but as "Subject" as well, Hegel says that: "The life of God and divine intelligence, then, can, if we like, be spoken of as love disporting with itself; but this idea falls into edification, and even sinks into insipidity, if it lacks the seriousness, the suffering, the patience, and the labor of the negative."[23] The meaning of these cryptic words is revealed by the paragraph which precedes them:

> The living substance, further, is that being which is truly subject, or, what is the same thing, is truly realized and actual (*wirklich*) solely in the process of positing itself, or in mediating with its own self its transitions from one state or position to the opposite. As subject it is pure and simple negativity,

and just on that account a process of splitting up what is simple and undifferentiated. . . . True reality is merely this process of reinstating self-identity, of reflecting into its own self in and from its other, and is not an original and primal unity as such, not an immediate unity as such. It is the process of its own becoming, the circle which presupposes its end as its purpose, and has its end for its beginning; it becomes concrete and actual only by being carried out, and by the end it involves.[24]

Negativity is simply the power and the process of the self-realization or the self-mediation of the "Subject" (the Hegelian Absolute), and, as such it is the true actuality (*Wirklichkeit*) of the world. By the end of *The Phenomenology of Mind*, we learn that "Mind" or "Spirit" (*Geist*) is the inherently negative or the negativity as found in Being *per se*; "i.e., it is absolute distinction from itself, is pure process of becoming its other."[25] This negative process of Subject or Spirit becoming its other is mythologized in pictorial thought (*Vorstellung*), Hegel tells us, by the image of the eternal generation of the Son, and Hegel can go so far as to construct a Trinity of Being in his desperate effort to give his metaphysics a Christian form.

Let us open our inquiry into Hegel by asking whether the "eternal negative" is not simply or finally a dialectical image of Christ. In the *Phenomenology*, the negative is the energy of thought, of the pure ego, of the Concept or Notion (*Begriff*). But the negative has not yet assumed a fully logical form in this work, and here it perhaps is given its fullest meaning in Hegel's kenotic understanding of the Incarnation. Hegel declares that pure thought has entered the sphere of actuality by the emptying, the *kenosis* of the eternal Being.[26] Employing the language of "kenosis"—which is admittedly the expression of a mythical or imaginative form of representation (*Vorstellung*)—Hegel attempts to unveil the deepest meaning of the Dialectic. There are two dimensions or sides of Spirit:

One is this, that substance empties itself of itself, and becomes self-consciousness; the other is the converse, that self-consciousness empties itself of itself and makes itself into the form of "thing," or makes itself universal self. Both sides have in this way met each other, and, in consequence, their true union has arisen. The relinquishment or "kenosis" on the part of the substance, its becoming self-consciousness, expresses the transition into the opposite, the unconscious transition of necessity, in other words, that it is *implicitly* self-consciousness. Conversely, the emptying of self-consciousness expresses this, that implicitly it is Universal Being. . . . For actual reality, or self-consciousness, and implicit being in the sense of substance are its [Spirit's] two moments; and by the reciprocity of their kenosis, each relinquishing or "emptying" itself of itself and becoming the other, spirit thus comes into existence as their unity.[27]

This is Hegel's tortured way of arriving at a dialectical identification of Subject and Object, of pure Self-Consciousness (Being-for-itself) and Being (Being-in-itself); but it is only meaningful by means of understanding negation as *kenosis*, and Hegel, despite himself, is driven to the mythical language of the Incarnation, a language that he himself believed must be negated to make way for "pure insight."[28]

In the course of this discussion, Hegel defines the Spirit that is the content of Absolute Religion as follows: "Spirit is knowledge of self in a state of alienation of self; Spirit is the Being which is the process of retaining identity with itself in its otherness."[29] Now I suggest that this understanding of Spirit embodies Hegel's deepest understanding of negativity, and that this is furthermore an authentic dialectical image of Christ, and that such an understanding is at least implicitly present in the "pure negativity" of the *Science of Logic*. Perhaps no work in the history of Western philosophy is as complex or as difficult as Hegel's *Logic*, but it is safe to say that for an understanding of this work everything depends upon an understanding of his method, its ground in negation, and the form which it assumes in the Dialectic. Hegel, in the Introduction, after having remarked upon the presence of a dialectical method in his *Phenomenology*, says that:

The one and only thing *for securing scientific progress* (and for quite *simple* insight into which, it is essential to strive)—is knowledge of the logical precept that Negation is just as much Affirmation as Negation, or that what is self-contradictory resolves itself not into nullity, into abstract Nothingness, but essentially only into the negation of its *particular* content, that such a negation is not an all-embracing Negation, but is *the negation of a definite somewhat* which abolishes itself, and thus is a definite negation. . . . Since what results, the negation, is a *definite* negation, it has a *content*. It is a new concept, but a higher, richer concept than that which preceded; for it has been enriched by the negation or opposite of that preceding concept, and thus contains it, but contains also more than it, and is the unity of it and its opposite.[30]

Even while confessing that the organization and structure of his logic do not belong to the content and body of the science of logic itself, and thus have only an historical value, Hegel nevertheless insists that his is the only true method: "This is already evident from the fact that the Method is no-ways different from its object and content; for it is the content in itself, *the Dialectic which it has in itself,* that moves it on."[31]

Consequently, it is quite true that Hegel's logic, unlike its Buddhist counterpart, is a dynamic or process logic; thought forges *ahead* by the negative which it carries within itself. It is this fact which also most clearly distinguishes Hegel's conception of dialectic from the earlier Western philosophical understanding of dialectic, as present in Plato and Kant, although, in his lectures on the history of philosophy, Hegel confesses that he has incorporated all of the fragments of Heraclitus into his own logic. Nor does Hegel hesitate to identify the most difficult aspect of the Dialectic—"the comprehension of the Unity of Opposites, or of the Positive in the Negative"[32]—with "speculative" knowledge. Pure logic is the realm of "shades," it is freed from all the concretions of sensory experience. Moreover Hegel identifies himself as an Idealist, defining philosophical Idealism as the recognition that the finite has no "veritable being," even while insisting that all philosophy and all religion are idealistic in this sense; "for religion equally with philosophy refuses to recognize in finitude a veritable being, or something ultimate and absolute, or non-posited, uncreated and eternal."[33] False philosophy and false religion are positivistic, they identify the given with the real, refusing to accept the reality of the Spirit, which is simply another name for absolute negativity. True negation is immediately opposed to "reality," or the given; and Hegel indirectly reveals that the source of his own understanding of negation lies in mystical religion:

"Qualation" or "Inqualation"—an expression belonging to Jacob Boehme's philosophy, a philosophy which goes deep but into a murky depth—means the movement of a quality (that of being sour, astringent, fiery, and so forth) in itself, insofar as it posits and confirms itself in its negative nature its *quale*) as opposed to an other and is its own restlessness, so that it is only by means of a struggle that it produces and maintains itself.[34]

If dialectic is the higher movement of Reason (*Vernunft*), as Hegel maintains, "where terms appearing absolutely distinct pass into one another because they are what they are, where the assumption of their separateness cancels itself,[35] then this movement is only possible through the act of negation, and through the identification of Reason as dialectical and negative.[36]

Technically, Hegel's organization of logic derives from its division into two "moments," moments deriving their existence from the opposition in consciousness between a subjective entity existing "for-itself" (*für sich*) and another similar objective entity existing "in-itself" (*an sich*). Logic is accordingly divided into subjective and objective logic, objective logic taking the place of the former metaphysics, and subjective logic is the logic of the Notion (*Begriff*)—"of Essence which has transcended its relation to any mere being, real or apparent, and in its determination is no longer external, but is the free, independent, and self-determining Subjective, or rather the Subject itself."[37] The first volume of Hegel's logic is devoted to objective logic, and its first part to an exposition of the doctrine of Being. Almost immediately Hegel effects an identification between Being and Nothing (pure Being equals pure Nothing), thus unveiling all too clearly the mystical ground of his system of logic. But it is in his discussion of finitude in the section on determinate Being (*Dasein*) that the mystical or religious ground of his method is most fully manifest. Here, finitude is defined as negation based on itself, a negation which is in abrupt opposition to its affirmative:

> When we say of things that they are finite, we mean thereby not only that they have a determinateness . . . that they are merely limited . . . but rather that Not-being constitutes their nature and their Being. Finite things are; but their relation to themselves is this, that, being negative, they are self-related,

and in this self-relation send themselves on beyond themselves and their being. They are, but the truth of this being is their end. The finite does not only change, like something in general, but it perishes; and its perishing is not merely contingent. . . . It is rather the very being of finite things, that they contain the seeds of perishing as their own Being-in-Self, and the hour of their birth is the hour of their death.[38]

Finitude is the refusal to move affirmatively to its own affirmative, the Infinite; "it is therefore posited inseparably from its Nothing, and every reconciliation with its Other, the affirmative, is thus precluded."[39] Understanding (*Verstand*) persists in this sorrow—or, should we say *Angst*?—of finitude by making not-being the determination of things, and also by making it enduring and absolute (here lies the attitude of the "positivist"). But through Reason (*Vernunft*), the opposition between the finite and the infinite is resolved: "This must be made evident; and the development of the finite shows that it is here that, because it is this contradiction, it collapses into itself, while at the same time it actually resolves the contradiction by showing, not that it is merely perishable and perishes, but that perishing, or Nothing, is not the last word, but perishes itself."[40]

When the infinite is posited in a qualitative relation of opposition to the finite as to its Other, Hegel insists that it must be called the "bad infinite" or the infinite of the Understanding (*Verstand*). In this form, the infinite remains in a state of absolute contradiction; while the infinite and the finite are artificially and falsely confined to two worlds or realms of being. Dialectically, however, the finite and the infinite are seen to posit each other, and thus to be inseparable. This is the "reciprocal determination" of the finite and the infinite; the finite is finite only with reference to the infinite, and the infinite is infinite only with reference to the finite: "the infinite is just a going beyond the finite; its determination makes it the negation of the finite; the finite, therefore, taken only as that which must be gone beyond, is in itself that self-negation which is infinity."[41] Therefore the Dialectic effects a *coincidentia oppositorum* between the finite and the infinite:

finite exists only as a passing beyond itself; it thus contains infinity, which is its Other. And, similarly, infinity exists only as a passing beyond finitude; it thus essentially contains its Other, and so is in itself its own Other. The infinite does not transcend the finite as a power existing external to the latter; rather it is the infinity of the finite to transcend itself.[42]

Previously, Hegel had established the thesis that a thing is transcended only insofar as it has come into unity with its opposite;[43] now we see that transcendence is neither otherness nor the transcendence of something.

The finite transcends itself in the infinite as negation of finitude; but the latter has for some time past been determinate Being determined as a Not-being. Thus, what is transcended in the negation is itself negation. So, on its side infinity is determined as the negative of finitude and therefore of determinateness in general; as a vacant beyond; its self-transcendence in finitude is a return from this empty flight; it is a negation of that beyond, which in itself it a negative.[44]

Dialectically, in both the finite and the infinite, we find the same negation of negation; but this is affirmation: "Thus, both infinite and finite are this movement which through negation returns to itself: they are in themselves only as mediation, and the affirmative of both contains the negation of both and is the negation of negation."[45] Hegel does not hesitate to speak of the relation between the finite and the infinite as an eternal process—and it might be noted that Hegel anticipated Nietzsche's understanding of Eternal Recurrence—just as he has no difficulty in joining his metaphysical predecessors in East and West by accepting the circle as the image of true infinity.

If one is to maintain that Hegel's vision of the true infinite is a Christian vision, then he must be prepared to admit that the Dialectic has led to a radically demythologized form of the Gospel. Let us note that recent French interpreters of Hegel, particularly the Marxists, have attempted to demonstrate that Hegel's thought derives in large measure from an early religious crisis of his life, a crisis arising from Hegel's realization of the death of God. In the *Phenomenology*, Hegel conceptualized this personal crisis in speaking of the "Unhappy Consciousness," a form of *Geist* wherein hope itself necessitates the absolute distance of the "beyond," and this because the "Unhappy Consciousness" cannot know that its wholly other object is at bottom "*its own self.*"[46] Ultimately, however, *Geist* is a movement of self that empties itself of self, becoming object, or Being-in-Self, thus establishing the necessity for a final identification of the opposites of Subject and Object, of Being-for-Self and Being-in-Self. By the conclusion of the *Phenomenology*, Hegel can speak of this process as the "Golgotha of Absolute Spirit," but his closing words insist that apart from this process *Geist* would be lifelessly enclosed within its own solitude. When Hegel speaks of the Golgotha of Spirit, just as when he employs the language of kenotic Christology, he is giving expression to his deepest vision of Spirit, to its absolute negativity. This vision of negativity negates or demythologizes the historic form of the Gospel, but in so doing it effects an identification of Christ with the world, of negativity with reality itself. Unlike Bultmann, but strangely anticipating Teilhard de Chardin, Hegel's dialectical negation of the transcendence of the Absolute creates a vision of the union of the Word and the world, wherein the Word becomes the power of the world, and a power finally leading to the End of the world.

Shortly after his discussion of the finite and the infinite in the *Logic*, Hegel says that "the negative in general contains the ground of Becoming, the unrest of self-movement: and in this sense the negative must be taken as the true negativity of the infinite.[47] The negative is the source of life and movement, but it is an infinite source, and an infinite source which is only realized or unfolded in the finite. As the *Logic* progresses, and we see the movement from Being to Essence to Notion, the movement itself always takes place by way of negation, each term being the negation of its predecessor, just as the self-identity of each term is always realized through the negation of itself. Yet as Hegel approaches the culmination of his logic in the Absolute Idea, the whole subject matter of the logic collapses into method: "Now the determinateness of the Idea and the whole evolution of this determinateness constituted the object of the Science of Logic, in whose course the Absolute Idea has emerged for itself; but, for itself, it has turned out to be this fact, that the determinateness has not the shape of a content, but is simply form. . . ."[48] This form is the absolute foundation of thought and its ultimate truth, it finally appears simply as dialectical method, a method emerging as the Notion which knows itself and has for object itself as the Absolute. What, then, is the Notion? The Notion is the eternal which is *in* and *for* itself, and thereby it is the unity of itself and its Other, a unity which appears as contradiction: "but the absolute unity of opposites in the Notion constitutes its essence, and therefore in its appearance and its relation to externality it manifests contradiction in its highest determinateness.[49] If the Notion is everything, as Hegel declares,[50] and its movement is the universal and the absolute activity, then that activity is simply contradiction, a dialectical contradiction, to be sure, and a contradiction which resolves itself in the "absolute unity" of the knowing Subject and the known Object. Its ground is what Hegel calls the "*dialectic* moment," a moment by which the original Subject determines itself out of itself to be its own Object or Other.[51] All too clearly this ground of the Dialectic is a logical conceptualization of the mystical idea that the Creation is a Fall of the Godhead, but the Dialectic transcends its mystical foundation by effecting a full dialectical identification between the Subject and its Other, an identification which parallels the Mahayana Buddhist identification of *nirvana* and *samsara*, but which also goes beyond this identification insofar as it allows the other to be *real*, and to be real precisely because it is the product of the *activity* of absolute negativity.

Hegel condemns "formal thought" because it makes contradiction unthinkable, and therefore it cannot move beyond the given: "but in truth the thinking of contradiction is the essential moment of the Notion."[52] At this point, however, we must ask the question, does Hegel's dialectical method ultimately allow the contradiction to be real? Is his understanding of the Absolute Idea the product of a premature coincidence of the opposites, premature because it refuses to allow the opposition to be wholly real, and this because it finally abandons negativity as the essential dialectical moment? John Findlay has spoken of the Hegelian dialectic as a "mystical game," a game in which Spirit simply "pretends" to be finite: "Spirit is the only reality, but it must confront itself with something seemingly alien, in order to see through its own self-deception, to become aware that it is the only reality."[53] If this were true, and it certainly is at least a half-truth, then the Hegelian dialectic would be little more than a Western analogue to the Hindu Vedanta, with its understanding of the world as the play (*lila*) of Brahman-Atman. But Hegel violates his own understanding of the Dialectic by allowing its final form to have a content. If the method culminates in the Absolute Idea, then dialectically the Idea must be "simply form," it can have no content which is susceptible of conceptualization. However, in the final pages of the *Logic*, Hegel adds the "content of cognition" to the dialectical method and thus extended the method into a "*system*."[54] Thereby he identified "the Idea" as a rational Idea, an identification reflecting the particularity of Hegel's own historical situation. Nevertheless, we must agree with Herbert Marcuse, who regards the idea of Reason as the undialectical element in Hegel's system.[55] So long as Spirit is known as Idea in a *rational* sense, the reality of the Object or the Other can only be provisional, the reality of contradiction must give way to a positive cognitive content, and pure negativity will thus cease to be absolute.

Hegel concludes his *Logic* by speaking of the "absolute liberation" which is effected by the "divine Notion."[56] Can we judge Hegel's understanding of liberation to be Christian? In the final paragraph on his excellent book on Hegel, Findlay goes so far as to answer this question in the affirmative: "We may also praise him, without absurdity, as in a sense the most Christian of thinkers, for while the official defenders of Christianity have usually borrowed their logic and the cast of their thought from Aristotle or from other sources, Hegel alone among thinkers has borrowed the whole cast of his thought from Christianity."[57] Now this is surely an absurd thesis in the pejorative sense, if we identify Hegel's thought with his "system." But, if, on the other hand, we identify his thought with his method, and identify his method as a dialectical movement of absolute negativity, then we need not hesitate to identify Hegel as a Christian thinker, providing, that is, that we are further willing to identify Christ as the absolute negativity who is the final source of the activity and the movement of existence. Such a confession may well be beyond the present powers of the theologian, but it points the way to an understanding of the reality of Christ in a world in which God is dead, just as it also unveils the uniqueness of Christianity. Authentic Christianity cannot grant the validity of a dichotomy between "body" and "soul," therefore it must negate the positive reality of the transmetaphysical "body" of the Buddha. The

Christian faith is possible only through *radical* negativity, a negativity that negates the world as the given, but a negativity that is only possible through the very reality of the world, and therefore a negativity which is rooted in contradiction. Ultimate Reality, or the Kingdom of God, must here be known both *by* and *as* negativity. Consequently the Jesus Christ, whose proclamation made incarnate the Kingdom in the present, whose Word transformed the transcendent into the immanent, is a Christ who is present only in a dialectical moment. And that moment is a moment of absolute negation, a negation occasioned by the very presence of the world which it must negate. May we hope that it is precisely the advent of a world in which God is dead that will yet occasion the deepest epiphany of Christ?

Notes

1. F. Th. Stcherbatsky, *The Conception of Buddhist Nirvana* (Leningrad, U.S.S.R., 1927), pp. 41–43. (Reprinted with same pagination by Mouton and Co., The Hague, 1965.)

2. F. Th. Stcherbatsky, *Buddhist Logic* (Leningrad, U.S.S.R., 1930), pp. 1, 2. (Reprinted with same pagination by Dover Publications, New York, 1962.)

3. Ibid., 1, 64ff., 71, 147.

4. Ibid., 1, 74, 147.

5. Ibid., 1, 419ff., 457.

6. Ibid., 1, 181ff.

7. Ibid., 1, 70.

8. Ibid., 1, 499.

9. Ibid., 1, 202.

10. Ibid., 1, 213–214.

11. Quoted and translated by Stcherbatsky, ibid., 1, 221.

12. Ibid., 1, 365.

13. Ibid., 1, 536.

14. Ibid., 1, 401.

15. Ibid., 1, 404.

16. Karl H. Potter, *Presuppositions of India's Philosophies* (Englewood Cliffs: Prentice-Hall, 1963), p. 141.

17. Stcherbatsky, *Buddhist Logic*, 2, 29.

18. Ibid., 2, 31–33.

19. Quoted and translated by Stcherbatsky, ibid., 1, 196.

20. Ibid., 1, 229–234.

21. Ibid., 1, 536, 485, 477.
22. Hegel, *Early Theological Writings*, trans. T. M. Knox and Richard Kroner (Chicago: University of Chicago Press, 1948), p. 316.
23. Hegel, *The Phenomenology of Mind*, trans. J. B. Baillie (London: George Allen and Unwin, 1931) p. 81.
24. Ibid., pp. 80–81.
25. Ibid., p. 766.
26. Ibid., p. 556.
27. Ibid., pp. 755–756.
28. Ibid., p. 553.
29. Ibid., p. 758.
30. Hegel, *Science of Logic*, trans. W. H. Johnston and L. G. Struthers (London: George Allen and Unwin, 1929), 1, 64–65.
31. Ibid., 1, 65.
32. Ibid., 1, 67.
33. Ibid., 1, 168.
34. Ibid., 1, 127.
35. Ibid., 1, 117.
36. Ibid., 1, 36.
37. Ibid., 1, 75.
38. Ibid., 1, 142.
39. Ibid.
40. Ibid., 1, 143–144.
41. Ibid., 1, 156.
42. Ibid., 1, 159.
43. Ibid., 1, 200.
44. Ibid., 1, 159.
45. Ibid., 1, 160.
46. Hegel, *Phenomenology of Mind,* pp. 255, 257.
47. Hegel, *Logic*, 1, 180.
48. Ibid., 2, 467.
49. Ibid., 2, 417.
50. Ibid., 2, 468.
51. Ibid., 2, 473.
52. Ibid., 2, 477.
53. John Findlay, *Hegel: A Re-Examination* (New York: Collier Books, 1962), p. 36.
54. Hegel, *Logic*, 2, 480.
55. Herbert Marcuse, *Reason and Revolution* (Boston: Beacon Press, 1960), p. xii.
56. Hegel, *Logic*, 2, 485.
57. Findlay, p. 359.

AMOR DEI*

Frank R. Harrison III

Events occurring in 1781 and 1923 were to affect radically theology and philosophy of religion. In 1781 the first edition of Immanuel Kant's *Critique of Pure Reason* appeared, and in 1923 the Vienna Circle was formed. I wish to examine briefly both events, and some consequences which ensued from them.

In the second half of the *Critique of Pure Reason*, Kant purports to show that all logical arguments for the existence of God are worthless. Put in other terms, Kant proposes that the existence of God can neither be proved nor disproved by any deductive means. In order to substantiate this claim, Kant distinguishes between three possible rational proofs for the existence of God. These are: (1) the ontological proof (*à la* René Descartes) which proceeds from the concept of perfection to the existence of a perfect thing, (2) the cosmological proof which proceeds from the fact that the cosmos exists to the maker of the cosmos, and (3) the physicoteleological proof which proceeds from observation of natural ordering in the cosmos to the source of that ordering. In effect, Kant points out that the cosmological and physicoteleological proofs must tacitly assume the ontological proof in order to reach the conclusion, "God exists." His reason is that the concept of God entails necessary existence, and only the ontological proof can guarantee this entailment. It is not enough to say that there is a cause of the cosmos. This cause, in order to be called "God," must necessarily exist. It is not enough to say that there is a source of ordering in the cosmos. This source of ordering, in order to be called "God," must necessarily exist—that is, the non-existence of God must be logically impossible.

There are only three possible ways to demonstrate the existence of God, and two of these assume the ontological argument; if Kant can show the ontological argument to be worthless, he

*This essay appeared in somewhat different form as "Knowing God," *Philosophy Today* 9 (Fall 1965): 200–210.

will have shown that all rational arguments are. How does he propose to do this?

The ontological argument, as Kant understands it, asserts that the concept of God must entail necessary existence. It would be contradictory to assert that some being was absolutely perfect and at the same time assert that this being did not necessarily exist. The concept of a merely *possible* absolutely perfect being, as contrasted with an *actual* absolutely perfect being, is self-stultifying. But an actual absolutely perfect being must necessarily exist, else it would not be absolutely perfect. Therefore, God necessarily exists as the absolutely perfect being. God is, then, *Ens realissimum*.

Kant criticizes this argument from two points. First, he draws the distinction between the concept, or definition, of a thing, and the thing itself. Surely, my concept, or definition, of "triangle" can be distinguished from any particular triangle. Now we can certainly give definitions of words like "triangle," e.g., "A figure formed by three lines intersecting by twos in three points, and so forming three angles." Nor is there any trick involved in giving a definition of the word "God," e.g., "A being whose non-existence is logically impossible." But so far we have only been defining the words, or if you please, concepts "triangle" and "God." Our problem arises when we attempt to go from the concept to that which is purportedly denoted by the concept. To define the word "God" as "A being whose non-existence is logically impossible" yields, as Kant says, "no insight into the conditions which make it necessary to regard the non-existence of a *thing* as absolutely unthinkable. . . ."[1]

To clarify this last point: if I grant that there are such things as triangles, then I must also grant that there necessarily exists three-sided objects of the sort defined by the word "triangle." Otherwise, I would contradict myself. But why must I grant that there are triangles? I may very well reject that there are triangles along with the property of their having three sides. And I would not contradict myself. Quite the opposite. Even the novice of logic knows the valid argument form "*modus tollens*." A particular instance of this argument form is, "If anything has three sides, then it is a triangle. But there are no triangles. Consequently, it follows as the night the day, that there are no three-sided things."

Apply this same procedure to the word, or concept, "God." If I grant that there is such a thing as God, then I must also grant there is something which necessarily exists, as defined by the word "God." Not to do this would be a contradiction. But why must I grant there is a God? I may very well reject that there is, and along with this also reject that there is a necessary being. As Kant says:

> "God is omnipotent" is a necessary judgment. The omnipotence cannot be rejected if we posit a Deity, that is an infinite being; for the two concepts are identical. But if we say, "There is no God," neither the omnipotence nor any other of its predicates is given; they are one and all rejected together with the subject, and there is therefore not the least contradiction in such a judgment. . . .[2]

To summarize Kant's first point we can say that any argument which purports to go from the definition of "X" to the existence of X is worthless. I could conclude, from the definition of something, that it exists only by begging the question. For I must already assume the existence of that very thing which I wish to prove existing.

Let us turn to Kant's second objection raised against the ontological argument. Kant holds that all statements must be either analytic or synthetic, and that all statements which asserted the existence of anything are synthetic. Furthermore, a statement is analytic when its denial is a contradictory statement,[3] and is synthetic when this is not the case. Thus, any existential statement is synthetic; i.e., its denial does not lead to a contradiction. Another way of putting this is that an analytic statement gives no new information about any particular thing, whereas a synthetic statement does.

But consider the statement, "there is a God," or simply, "God exists." This statement must also be either analytic or synthetic. If analytic, the concept of "existence" adds nothing to our concept of "God," and thus to deny that God exists is not to deny one predicate of God, but all of them. And, as we have seen from Kant's first point against the ontological argument, no contradiction arises. Or the statement, "there is a God," or "God exists," is synthetic. If this were the case, the concept of existence would have to be a descriptive predicate which added something to the concept of God. But: " 'Being' is obviously not a real predicate; that is, it is not a concept of something which could be added to the concept of a thing. It is merely the positing of a thing, or of certain determinations, as existing in themselves."[4] To say, "God exists," is to say, "there is some X, such that X is first cause, and X is the source of all order, and X is omnipresent, and. . ." *etc.* Thus to deny the statement, "God exists" is not to deny the property of existence, and not, say, omnipresence. It is simply a shorthand way of denying all the predicates commonly attributed to God—that is to deny God.

Thus we cannot logically demonstrate the existence of God by means of the ontological argument. But since all other purported demonstrations of God's existence assume the validity of this argument, we cannot logically demonstrate the existence of God. Therefore, we can never prove—or disprove for that matter— whether anything does or does not actually correspond to our concept of God.

However, the concept of God is still useful as a regulative principle for moral action and for our thinking about the world. Though we cannot logically demonstrate the existence of God, we have a very practical need to assume His existence. If we did not make such an assumption, moral action would be impossible, as would *meaningful* moral judgments. But there is moral action, and there are meaningful moral judgments. Thus we must assume, according to Kant, that God does exist, and the statement, "there is a God," is true in some not overly clear sense of the word "true."

In the line of succession from Kant we find the post-Kantian period of Romanticism and anti-intellectualism, Fichte and Schelling, and finally in our own day Paul Tillich. To paraphrase Bowman Clarke, Kant started by attempting to show that we could neither logically prove nor disprove the statement, "there is a God." Nevertheless, as a regulative principle of practical reason the statement was still meaningful, still true. Tillich asserts that we cannot even say, "there is a God," or "God exists." We cannot even say, "there is not a God," or "God does not exist." In doing this, Tillich "removes the problem of God to the realm of faith, the state of being ultimately concerned, making God 'the element of ultimacy' in any ultimate concern. This is the 'God above God' which transcends theism in all its forms."[5]

According to Tillich, we can say *nothing* literally meaningful about God, much less demonstrate His existence. But this is to assert that we know nothing about God in any literal way. And yet He is the element of ultimacy in any ultimate concern. How curious it is that something of which in principle nothing can be known could be of such importance to our individual lives.

But these are not the only developments which have molded the contemporary scene in theology and philosophy of religion. I have already mentioned in passing the founding of the Vienna Circle in 1923. Under the guidance of Moritz Schlick, the members of the Circle were primarily interested in the problem of the meaning of statements, as contrasted with the truth or falsity of any particular statement. After all, in order to say whether any statement is true or false, one must first know what that statement means. What is required is a concise and clear criterion of meaning. Any utterance which does not meet the requirements of the criterion is counted as cognitively meaningless, although such an utterance might have rhetorical or poetical uses.

In developing such a criterion the first step taken was to catalogue all statements into one of two categories, but not both. First there are observational statements, i.e., statements which purport to assert something about such things as sealing wax, cabbages and kings. "I am now reading a paper," "the earth has one moon," "the sky fell on Chicken Little's head" are examples of empirical statements. Also included in this category are statements which themselves do not assert anything directly about observable phenomena, but which allow us to make predictions about such phenomena. Examples of these would be Heisenberg's equations, or those of Schrödinger. These very general statements, when conjoined with particular observational statements, permit us to forecast future occurrences of varying sorts. The actual occurrence of the predicted phenomena will constitute verifying evidence for these very general statements. Failure of the predicted events to occur will constitute falsifying evidence. Let us refer to both of these types of statements as empirical.

When are empirical statements meaningful? Or what is the meaning of an empirical statement? To ask this question is to ask under what conditions would such a statement count as true, and under what conditions would it count as false. Notice that we are not asking whether any particular empirical statement is actually true or not. We are saying that in order for any empirical statement to be meaningful, we must be able to say under what *conditions* that statement would be true, and under what *conditions* it would be false. It must be logically possible to indicate what kind of evidence, if actually found, would prove the statement true. And it must be logically possible to indicate what kind of evidence, if actually found, would prove the statement false. Or, in terms of logic, an empirical statement is one which can be denied without contradiction.

The second general category of meaningful statements is that of analytic statements. The best examples of these are provided by mathematics and logic. "5 + 7 = 12," "the sum of the angles of a Euclidian triangle is 180°," "Dave is either a good student or he isn't," are but a few examples. There are, however, other analytic statements. Examples of these are, "all bachelors are unmarried men," "man is a featherless biped," two brothers are male siblings," and so on. The claim made by the Vienna Circle was that the meanings of these statements depend solely on our arbitrary use of the words in the various statements. To phrase this in a somewhat different manner, it could be said that the conditions of the truth or falsity of such statements depend upon the conventions of the linguistic system to which they belong. Thus, in order to know the statement "all bachelors are unmarried men" is both meaningful and true, we do not have to sojourn into the world observing cases of men who are bachelors. We know the statement is meaningful and true because of the conventional use of "bachelors" and "unmarried men." Such statements, so the claim goes, say nothing about the world of cabbages and kings and, consequently, the world in no way can be counted as providing a means for either verifying or falsifying them. No appeal to empirical evidence is needed or warranted.

With this distinction of meaningful statements at hand, the members of the Vienna Circle turned their attention to such assertions as "God exists," or "there is a God." Is this a cognitively meaningful statement or not? The first step in this linguistic game is to ascertain what the assertor intends by his utterance, "God exists." It would certainly seem that he is making some sort of factual, or empirical claim. After all, the assertion "God exists" looks very much like "Dave exists." But, we are told that "God exists" cannot be counted among cognitively meaningful empirical statements. Why? Because the assertor, the full-blooded religious man, will allow nothing to count against the truth of the assertion. In principle, there is no empirical evidence which he would accept as falsifying the claim "God exists." Of course, the religious man may say that some observable phenomena *seem* to count against the truth of the assertion "God exists." There are, for example, enormous amounts of seemingly needless pain suffered by seemingly innocent people. But the religious man would say we do not know the entire story. Only God could know that. Or he might claim that since we have all sinned through the fall of Adam, we all deserve to suffer. Or he might say that suffering now guarantees our pie in the sky by-and-by. And any other observable phenomena which mitigated against the purported truth of "God exists" would be treated in similar ways.

In a word, the religious man would permit nothing to count against the truth of the assertion "God exists." But, according to the criterion of meaning purposed by the Vienna Circle, a sentence that denies nothing can never assert something. This is to say that "God exists" cannot be counted as a cognitively meaningful empirical statement.

If the assertion "God exists" is cognitively meaningful and it is not an empirical statement, then it must be an analytic statement. This being the case, we would not have to worry about the problem of its non-falsifiability. Furthermore, we would know that the assertion, if true, is necessarily true. That is, we would know that there could never be any condition, or set of conditions, which would falsify it. Perhaps now our problems are over. Perhaps now we can say the assertion "God exists" is, after all, meaningful and get on with other things. But this is not the happy solution which at first it might appear to be. For if the assertion "God exists" is to be counted as analytic, there need not be any existing being to which the word "God" refers. If analytic and if true, then the assertion "God exists" is true simply in virtue of the ways in which we conventionally use the words "God" and "exist." That is to say, the assertion "God exists" would only reflect something about our arbitrary rules of language. A religious man, however, wants to say more than this. Yet from the point of view of the Vienna Circle, if the attempt to claim more is made, there will be the immediate ensuance of literal non-sense.

Let me suggest that J. N. Findlay clearly embodies this view. Consider the following passage:

> The religious frame of mind seems, in fact to be in a quandry; it seems invincibly determined both to eat its cake and have it. It desires the Divine Existence both to have the inescapable character which can, on modern views, only be found where truth reflects an arbitrary convention, and also the character of "making a real difference" which is only possible where truth doesn't have this merely linguistic basis. We may accordingly deny that modern approaches allow us to remain agnostically poised in regard to God: they force us to come down on the atheistic side. For if God is to satisfy religious claims and needs, he must be a being in every way inescapable, One whose existence and whose possession of certain excellences we cannot possibly conceive away. And modern views make it selfevidently absurd (if they don't make it ungrammatical) to speak of such a Being and attribute existence to him.[6]

If the assertion "God exists" is not a cognitively meaningful empirical statement, or an analytic statement, then what is it? In his recent book, *The Problem of Religious Knowledge*,[7] Professor Blackstone carefully outlines and discusses several alternatives. I wish to mention two of these; *viz.*, the positions of A. J. Ayer and R. B. Braithwaite.

Professor Ayer, having maintained that there is "no possibility of demonstrating the existence of a God," proceeds to maintain that the utterance "God exists" is cognitively meaningless.[8] Nevertheless, it does serve as an expression of feeling. For example, the utterance "ouch" is cognitively meaningless. It is just not the sort of thing, given our language, which could count as being either true or false. But "ouch" may express a feeling. The utterances "God exists" and "ouch" are just alike in this respect. But such utterances as "ouch" may also act in another way. They may serve to arouse certain feelings in other persons. If the aroused feeling is strong enough, other persons may even be moved to action. Suppose a person wanted the sympathetic attention of someone. He might well utter "ouch" in a pathetic sort of way, thereby stimulating someone to act in a desired way, *viz.*, give him sympathetic attention. The utterance "God exists" may also be employed in similar ways. It may also be used to get people to act in desired ways. In short, then, Ayer interprets "God exists" in the same way as "ouch." Both are simply emotive ejaculations.

Accepting the position of the Vienna Circle, Professor Braithwaite takes a different tack than Ayer in regards to religious language.[9] The utterance "God exists" is not to be counted as either an analytic statement or as a straightforward empirical statement. It is suggested that "God exists" has some use in our language, and therefore a meaning in some sense of "meaning." The meaning of the utterance "God exists" is given in terms of its use, and its use is to assert the intention of the assertor to follow a certain behavior pattern. Such an utterance not only refers to the intentions of the assertor, but also to a body of stories, or myths. These myths need not be believed, or even be consistent with one another. The requirement is that they have a meaning and be thought about, for the use of these myths is to help one pursue a way of life—a fairly specific behavior pattern. Thus religious myths are not to be counted as any sort of cognitive evidence for religious beliefs. Rather they are to be understood as having a psychological and causal efficacy on our individual actions. These myths are to be viewed as psychological supports for a fairly particular behavior pattern that the religious man has asserted he is going to follow. Thus, "God exists" is interpreted as an "assertion of an intention to carry out a certain behavior policy, subsumable under a sufficiently general principle to be a moral one, together with the implicit or explicit statement, but not the assertion, of certain stories."[10]

Both the influence of Kant and the Vienna Circle have led to philosophical positions denying the possibility of any rational proof of the existence of God, denying any possible rational knowledge of God. What is the logical import of such a claim? One interpretation would be this. No definite description, or characterization, of the word "God" can be given such that this description would satisfy what a Christian usually means by "God," and at the same time allow the statement, "there is a God," to be deducible in some axiomatic system. To put this in another way: If we can give a definite description for the word "God" such that it is satisfactory to the Christian tradition, then we cannot prove the statement, "there is a God." If, on the other hand, we can prove the statement, "there is a God," we cannot give a definite description of "God" such that it is satisfactory for Christian claims.

Bowman Clarke has suggested an ingenious way of avoiding this situation.[11] It is also, in different terms, the proposal of St. Thomas Aquinas. The following points are required. A formalized language must be developed such that (1) the statement "there is a God" is deducible from the rules of the language. (2) The formalized language must be such that it allows for the formation of any descriptive statement, true or false, we wish to assert about the empirical world. (3) The formalized language must guarantee mathematics. (4) The word "God" is to be thought of as the name of an individual for which a definite description can be given. (5) This definite description is to be formulated in terms of primitive predicates, i.e., predicates used in describing the empirical world.

Some interesting results would follow from such a formalized language. The statement "there is a God" is necessarily true in the system. By this I mean that it is deducible from the rules of the system alone. It is also a meaningful statement on two counts. First, it is deducible from the rules, and second the name "God" is given a definite description of the kind already mentioned. Further, since the statement "there is a God" is necessarily true, it is implied by *any* statement which can be formulated according to the rules of the language. Let me put this into more traditional terms. If any particular thing exists, then so does God. This is the import of St. Thomas's *Quinque Viae*. If there is at least one movable thing, God exists. If there is at least one contingent thing, God exists—and so on. Of course, God's existence does not depend on their being some particular thing which exists. But any particular thing which exists depends on God's existence. Thus, God is the necessary condition for any particular existing thing, though He is not the immediate sufficient condition.[12]

Our formalized language must be one in which the traditional attributes of God are also derivable. Traditionally, and here I am referring specifically to the Christian tradition, God is said to be omnipresent. What does this mean? As a first approximation someone might say that it means God is everywhere at once, and not at any one particular place at any one particular time. This, however, does not make much sense unless we know what is to count as an instance of a particular place and of a particular time.[13] Hopefully these would be defined in terms of our primitive predicates. Saying that God is omnipresent may then turn out to be asserting that God is the necessary condition for any element definable in the terms of the rules of the formalized language and its primitive predicates. To quote Clarke: "As the necessary condition of any finite segment, God could be thought of as the perfect object—that is, every creature without qualification must take account of him."[14] The same sort of thing must be carried through with the notions of simplicity, perfection, omniscience, omnipotence, goodness, and so on.

The theoretical advantages of such a formalized language are obvious at once. In the first place, we avoid Kant's criticism that existence is not a predicate. To say that God necessarily exists is to say the statement "there is a God" is deducible from the rules of the system. Thus, we are not attempting to predicate existence to God. We are not, however, simply deducing an uninterpreted statement. In a word, we are not arguing from the concept of God to the object. This is avoided by defining the name of the individual, "God," in terms of primitive predicates which also characterize the empirical world. In the second place, we avoid the position of the Vienna Circle and the various ramifications issuing from it. The statement "there is a God" is certainly meaningful in that it is deducible from the rules of the formalized language, and in that the name "God" is defined in the terms of the primitive predicates of the system. Furthermore, the statement "there is a God" turns out to be necessarily true and also related to contingent statements as their necessary condition.

I am not claiming that a formalized language such as I have suggested would be an easy thing to develop. To formalize just the rules for mathematics would take somewhat longer than one rainy afternoon, or winter night. The finished work of the entire language may well look like a crossbreed between *Principia Mathematica* and *Summa Theologicae*—with a few other strains appearing here and there. But all of this is beside the point. The central question is simply can such a program be carried through? Is it logically possible? There is every reason to believe it is. The tasks of the theologian and philosopher of religion now become clear. They are to help carry through the formalization of the language which I have described.

Let us assume that our formalized language has been developed, that we can deduce the statement "there is a God," that we can give the required sort of definite description to the name "God," and the like. At once we should notice how highly abstract statements like "there is a God," "God is omnipresent," "God is omniscient," are. For example, such statements tell me nothing in particular about my concrete relation to God. I know that He is the necessary condition for my existence. But He is also the necessary condition for the existence of anything else. "God is omniscient" tells me that God is the necessary condition for all true statements. But this does not inform me which particular statements are true and which are not in any concrete case. In more Thomistic terms, I know *that* God is, that He is the necessary condition for all particular existing things, and all truth. But I do not know *what* He is in any concrete way.

If we define "knowledge" as "that which can be meaningfully asserted in accordance with the rules of our formalized language," then we must admit a basic agnostic position concerning the nature, or essence, of God. Or we might want to distinguish between two uses of "knowledge." We may call the first "knowledge by description." By this we would understand "that which can be meaningfully asserted in accordance with the rules of our formalized language." The second may be referred to as "knowledge by acquaintance." Such knowledge is, in principle, not expressible in accordance with the rules of our language, which is to say such knowledge is linguistically non-discursive. It is a direct apprehension, or encounter, as such. It is exactly at this point that the concept of mysticism, or *amor Dei*, becomes paramount.

In order to achieve some clarity, allow me to construct an example. Let us suppose that I have a very good friend. He is, as Aristotle would say, an alter ego. He is not simply a business partner, or a "drinking buddy." My friend, then, is not simply an object from which I can gain some personal advantage. He, for me, is other than a convenient thing, a convenient possession. However, I can say many things about him as an object. I can describe his height, weight, the color of his eyes. I can say whether he is standing up or sitting down, whether he is asleep or awake. There are assertions I can make about his intellect, given certain criteria such as I.Q. tests, college examinations, and the like. I can describe his reaction to various stimuli, and predict his future actions in relation to similar stimuli. I can assert that he is a person, as opposed to some other sort of object. All of this can be done within the framework of descriptive language.

But when all is said and done, I still have not described my friend as such. I have only described an object, a thing, in my physical environment. Wherein is my friend, as friend, in this description? And yet, I wish to say that I know—in some sense of "know"—my friend as other than an object, or thing. I have, as it were, come face to face with him *other than as an object. Ubi desinit cognitio . . . ibi statim dilectio*[15]—"where knowledge fails, love can still advance," is the formula used by St. Thomas. A more modern writer, Antoine de Saint-Exupéry, puts it in the following way. "—Adieu, dit le renard. Voici mon secret. Il est très simple: on ne voit bien qu'avec le coeur. L'essentiel est invisible pour les yeux."[16] And: "Le langage est source de malentendus."[17] Thus, I can say that I know my friend as a thing, or object, describable in statements which are in accordance with the rules of our formalized language. I, however, love my friend, as friend, and this is not expressible in terms of descriptive statements. It is a direct relationship, or activity, into which we enter. And, as such, it unites us as two persons with one will—*eadem velle*, to will the same thing.

Even though this relation is not expressible in descriptive language, nevertheless, it is necessary that I should be able to say something descriptively about the person who is my friend. If it were not, I could not love him as my friend. For how could anyone possibly love another unless there were some descriptive knowledge of the beloved? If I know nothing descriptively about a person, a fortiori, I do not even know he is a person. We can never love the completely unknown, the completely undescribable. In general, let us say that some literal, descriptive knowledge of X is a necessary, but not sufficient, condition for loving X. This has a corollary. Because descriptive knowledge is not a sufficient condition for loving a person, we may love someone who is very imperfectly known. Again, to cite St. Thomas: "It is enough for the perfection of love that the thing be loved such as it is apprehended in itself, and this is the reason it happens that something is loved more than it is known, because that something can be perfectly loved even though it is not perfectly known."[18]

There are at least two other necessary conditions which must be fulfilled. First, I must want to love my friend. I can certainly know a great deal about a person, be able to say a great deal about him, and still not consider him as a friend. Indeed, I might do just the reverse; that is, definitely not want him to be my friend. Therefore, I must want a person to be my friend, I must trust in his goodness as a friend, before he can actually become my friend. Second, he must want me to become his friend. No matter how much I know about a person, no matter how much I want to become his friend; nevertheless, he might not want to enter into such a relation with me. In order to enter into this direct apprehension of a person, he must reveal himself to me other than as an object, or thing.

Thus, in the example of two people, who enter in the relation of love, we find several necessary conditions which must be fulfilled. (1) I must have some knowledge of the person; that is, I must be able to say something descriptively about him. (2) I must want to be his friend. I do not want to treat him as a thing for my own personal gains, benefits or pleasures. (3) He must allow me to enter into this relation with him. He must reveal himself to me other than simply as an object in my physical environment. I do not claim that this list of conditions is exhaustive, but these are certainly necessary.

Similiter est dicendum circa amorem Dei.

I can love God wholly, while only knowing Him imperfectly. By this I understand that I can enter into a concrete relation with God, even though my knowledge of Him is highly abstract. In order to enter into this relation I must come, as it were, face-to-face with God. I must encounter Him. But in order to do this I must have some knowledge of what I am to encounter. This is why a necessary condition for my love of God is that I first know something literally true about Him. But there are two other necessary conditions for this relation, or activity, of love. I must want to love God, and He must allow me to love Him. He must show Himself to me. In more traditional terms, I must have faith in God, and He must reveal Himself to me.

I must have faith in God, but a faith based on my knowledge of God as the necessary condition for all existing things and for all true statements. My faith, then, is not irrational. It is a personal trust in, or dependence on, God. But it is a trust based on my knowledge of Him. Further, God must reveal Himself to me. That is, He must allow me to love Him, to commit myself to Him in a relation of love. In Christian theology, this last requirement is set forth in the doctrine of the Incarnation. It is the Incarnation which allows man to become a friend of God. The Incarnation guarantees the revealment of God to those who wish to love Him, to become united with Him.

I have suggested three necessary conditions for the activity of X loving Y, where X and Y may be either persons or a person and God. There well may be other such conditions. But, while talking about these necessary conditions, I have said little about the concrete relation of love itself. The reason for this is that this relation, as a concrete activity between two persons or a person and God, is non-describable or linguistically non-discursive. Such an activity may be shown or expressed, but it is not describable. And yet the activity of love is essential for an individual's unique apprehension of God. It is, therefore, the case that Christianity must find its completion in the activity of love. For the end of the Christian is to become united with God through the love of God —*amor Dei*—that love which is also reflected in one person's love for his fellow being—*amor amicī*.

> Though I speak with the tongues of men and of angels, and have not love, I am become as sounding brass, or a tinkling cymbal.
> And though I have the gift of prophecy, and understanding all mysteries, and all knowledge; and though I have all faith, so that I could remove mountains, and have not love, I am nothing.
> . . . .
> And now abideth faith, hope, love, these three; but the greatest of these is love.[19]

Notes

1. Immanuel Kant, *Critique of Pure Reason*, trans. Norman Kemp Smith (London: Macmillan Press, 1959), A 594–595, B 622–623.

2. Ibid.

3. Ibid., A 150–151, B 191.

4. Ibid., A 598–599, B 626–627.

5. Bowman L. Clarke, "God and the Symbolic in Tillich," *Anglican Theological Review* (July 1961): 3–12.

6. Antony Flew and Alasdair MacIntyre, eds., *New Essays in Philosophical Theology* (London: SCM Press, 1955), p. 54–55.

7. William T. Blackstone, *The Problem of Religious Knowledge* (Englewood Cliffs: Prentice–Hall, 1963).

8. Alfred J. Ayer, *Language, Truth and Logic* (New York: Dover Publications, Inc.), pp. 114–116.

9. R. B. Braithwaite, "An Empiricists's View of the Nature of Religious Belief," Eddington Memorial Lectures, 1955.

10. Ibid., p. 32.

11. See Professor Clarke's essay in this volume.

12. F. R. Harrison, "Some Brief Remarks Concerning the *Quinque Viae* of St. Thomas," *Franciscan Studies* 21 (1961): 80–93.

13. This would require a development of a "calculus of individuals."

14. Clarke, "God and the Symbolic in Tillich," p. 10.

15. *Summa Theologicae* (Parma edition), I–II, q 27, a 4, ad 1.

16. Antoine de Saint-Exupéry, *Le Petit Prince* (New York: Harcourt, Brace and Company, 1943), p. 71.

17. Ibid., p. 67.

18. *Summa Theologicae* (Parma edition), I–II, q 26, a 2 and ad 2; q 28, a 2.

19. I Corinthians 13:1, 2, 13.

LINGUISTIC ANALYSIS OF RELIGIOUS LANGUAGE: A PROFUSION OF CONFUSION

R. David Broiles

The problem of religious knowledge, in the context of contemporary philosophical analysis, is basically this: no one has any. The problem of religious language, in the same context, is this: can we find an excuse for uttering these sentences we apparently have no business saying? I propose to examine one answer to this problem, that of R. M. Hare who starts from the assumption that no one has any religious knowledge and moves to the contention that no one can have any religious knowledge. It will be argued that Hare's position is unsound.

I will begin by referring to Antony Flew's discussion of "Theology and Falsification." Flew uses a parable (see Blackstone's essay), to illustrate how what starts out as an assertion that something exists may be reduced step by step to an altogether different status. Assertions can be so qualified until they no longer assert anything. The process of qualification can make them compatible with the existence of any state of affairs. Thus Flew maintains that if there is nothing which a putative assertion denies then there is nothing which it asserts either, and so it is really not an assertion. This is the falsifiability criterion.

As Flew sees it, many apparent religious statements fail this test. The statements "God loves us" and "God exists" are often literally qualified to death, i.e., they are eroded by qualifications until they are not assertions at all. In keeping with the "sophisticated" character of the parable, Flew interprets "God loves us" to mean that God loves us as a father loves his children. But then we consider the suffering in the world. Consider a child dying of inoperable cancer of the throat: the earthly father does everything in his power to save the child, but the Heavenly Father reveals no obvious sign of concern. Certainly this is incompatible with God loving us like a father. So "God loves us" is qualified, and we say his love is not like human love. At this, Flew issues this challenge: "What would have to occur or to have occurred to constitute for you a disproof of the love of, or of the existence of, God?"[1]

It is not altogether in line with the purpose of this paper to examine the merits of the falsifiability criterion. It does seem to me, however, that anyone who believes that the events of the world are evidence for the belief in God's existence should be able to say what events would have to occur in order for this belief to be considered unwarranted. It also seems to me that if religious statements are to be of any *significance* in our lives, that they will have to be incompatible with the occurrence of certain things in the world. Later in the paper I shall try to make clear this contention that any statement that denies nothing, that is, is compatible with anything that happens, cannot be of any significance with regard to how we should live our lives. For the present, however, I wish to consider what I hope is at least a fairly typical response to Flew's challenge. What is so interesting about this kind of response, and why I have singled it out for consideration, is that it allows Flew to carry the day and agrees that religious statements are non-assertive. Nothing does count against their truth—simply because they are not true. In fact, they are neither true nor false, and it is a mistake to treat them as though they were.

The response to the falsifiability criterion that I want to consider is R. M. Hare's. In his reply to Flew, Hare argues that religion is a *blik*. Religious statements are expressions of *bliks*. Now one of the reasons I am examining Hare's position is because of his use of the word "*blik*." For those not familiar with Hare's position, "*blik*" is a meaningless term. Thus, you can consider "*blik*" as a variable, and if you don't like "*blik*," you might say that religious statements are convictional statements, discernment-commitment statements, attitude statements, emotive statements, or disguised moral statements. I am not concerned with the arguments one would give for any one of these different interpretations of religious statements, but rather with the belief that religious statements are not assertive and thus must be some other type of statement. Hare believes that Flew is completely victorious on the grounds that he has marked out for attack. But Flew's mistake is in his misconception of the

nature of religion. Flew, Hare points out, regards religious talk
as some sort of *explanation*, as scientists are accustomed to use
the word. As such, "*religion would obviously be ludicrous.*"[2] We
no longer believe in God as an atlas." Religion, Hare contends,
is not an explanation, but a *blik*. *Bliks* are not explanations, but
without a *blik* there can be no explanation; for it is by our *bliks*
that we decide what is and what is not an explanation.

Hare illustrates what a *blik* is by means of a parable.

> A certain lunatic is convinced that all dons want to murder
> him. His friends introduce him to all the mildest and most
> respectable dons that they can find, and after each of them
> has retired, they say, "You see, he doesn't really want to mur-
> der you; he spoke to you in a most cordial manner; surely you
> are convinced now?" But the lunatic replies, "Yes, but that
> was only his diabolical cunning; he's really plotting against me
> the whole time; I know it I tell you." However many kindly
> dons are produced, the reaction is still the same.[3]

Hare believes that this parable points out what *bliks* are. We say
of the man that he is deluded. But, Hare asks, what is he deluded
about? Hare argues, that on Flew's criterion, the lunatic is not
deluded about the truth or falsity of an assertion. For nothing
the dons do will count against his theory that the dons are out
to kill him. Therefore, his theory, on the falsifiability criterion,
asserts nothing. But it does not follow that because his belief is
non-cognitive, that is, neither true nor false, that the belief *makes
no difference*. It is this non-cognitive point of view, this *blik*, that
makes a difference in the lunatic's action towards dons from the
actions of others who have a sane *blik* about dons. It is important
to realize, Hare argues, that we have the right *blik*, not just no
blik at all; "for there must be two sides to any argument—if he
has the wrong *blik*, then those who are right about dons must
have the right one."[4]

From this Hare concludes that religion is a *blik*. The statements of religion are neither true nor false, for nothing counts
against their truth. But they do make a difference in our lives—
and in this sense it is incorrect to say they are meaningless.

Let us now look at Hare's argument in greater detail. First
of all, let us consider Hare's concession to Flew that religious

statements are not assertive. In conceding to Flew that there are no conditions that would count against the statement "God exists," Hare has made an interesting confession. And I say this is a confession, for it is certainly not a factual observation. Hare has said that nothing will count against the statement "God exists" as he understands it. But certainly this is not the case with many classical theologians and philosophers. Take Descartes as an example. In the "Third Meditation," Descartes tries to prove the existence of God. Descartes conceives of God as all-powerful and all-good. Now, would anything count against this conception of God? Descartes believes that the existence of error and evil count against this conception of God. Consequently, the Fourth Meditation is devoted solely to removing these two problems. Descartes points out that men make errors because they have a free will that surpasses their understanding, and that what we consider natural evil may not be evil when seen in the whole scheme of things. Descartes, I take it, would consider that there are conditions that would count against the belief, in an all-powerful and all-good God—for instance, the fact of the existence of evil in the world. This would count against our belief, were Descartes not able to point out how the existence of evil and error is compatible with God's existence. Descartes believes he is asserting something. What he is saying is either true or false.

Further, the existence of God in Descartes's system serves as an *explanation* of certain things in the world. Descartes's argument, in the Third Meditation, is: since something cannot come from nothing, and since the cause of an idea must have at least as much reality as the idea represents, and since I have an idea of an infinitely perfect being, and since I could not be the cause of this idea, then an infinitely perfect being exists as the cause of this idea. That is, how can I *explain* the presence of this idea of God? It can only be explained if God exists as the cause of the idea. Not only is God the cause of my idea of him, but, Descartes adds, he is the creator and sustainer of my existence. It seems obvious that Descartes believed the proposition "God exists" to be true and also to be an explanation of certain phenomena.

How is it that Hare and Descartes differ so? Hare believes exactly the opposite of Descartes—that religious statements are not assertive and not explanations. I believe that even Hare would have to admit that Descartes was making an assertion and trying to give a causal explanation. Hare would be wrong if he said that Descartes was merely expressing a *blik*. But if what I have said is true, then it is incorrect to say that the sentence "God exists" is a *blik*. It is not a *blik* for Descartes, and to say so is to misinterpret Descartes.

Now, how can the same sentence be assertive for one man and not so for the other. I think the key to this problem is found in Hare's statement that to regard such talk as some sort of explanation "would obviously be ludicrous." And further, he asserts, "we no longer believe in God as an Atlas. . . ." What happened in the three hundred and fourteen years between the *Meditations* and the *New Essays in Philosophical Theology*? Certainly I cannot hope to cover this period in the space of one paper. But let me make these observations. Many contemporary philosophers hold that the possibility of proving the existence of God has been virtually annihilated by the criticisms of such men as Hume and Kant. In the tradition of English philosophy, Hume has certainly carried the day over Descartes with regard to the problem of our knowledge of God's existence. Hare acknowledges a debt to Hume and his insights on religion. How was Hume of service to Hare in the latter's formulation of religious beliefs as *bliks*? In reference to our considerations of Descartes, Hume argued, and rather effectively, that if there is evil in the world and God is all-good, then he is not all-powerful; and if he is all-powerful, and there is evil in the world, then he is not all-good. Since Descartes admits the existence of evil, it is impossible for Descartes' God, as all-powerful and all-good, to exist. The existence of evil is *incompatible* with the existence of a God of this nature. That is to say, the existence of a Being who can do anything and is completely good *denies* the possibility of the existence of evil. Here is a condition that would disprove the statement "God exists," when God is thought to have a certain nature.

I have mentioned Hume and Descartes as classical examples of the controversies that have arisen in trying to prove the existence of God. But, and what is more important, I mention this type of controversy because I believe it illuminates Hare's statement to the effect that any conception of God's existence as some sort of explanation is "obviously ludicrous." For what I want to contend is that the most Hare means by "ludicrous" is that such attempts are always failures. And they fail because they are false. And they are false because certain phenomena in the world are incompatible with the existence of such a Being as Descartes has in mind.

Hare believes that any argument for the existence of God, as classically conceived, is doomed to failure. It is doomed to failure because such a conception is incompatible with certain phenomena in the world, e.g., evil. But rather than say that it is false that God exists, Hare says that nothing counts against God's existence. He falls back on Flew's falsifiability criterion and by its means saves religion from being "ludicrous." I am using Hare as an example to illustrate my first statement of this paper: that the problem of religious knowledge, in the context of contemporary philosophical analysis, is that there isn't any knowledge. Now I want to try to make clear the argument that leads from the admission that there is no religious knowledge to the conclusion that religious utterances express *bliks*. The argument, briefly stated, goes as follows.

First argument: (1) The conclusion of the classical arguments for the existence of God is false if it is not qualified. (2) If we do not qualify the arguments then we will have to give up our religious beliefs or believe something that is false. (3) We do not want to give up our religious beliefs, for they are important to us, and we do not want to believe something that is false. (4) Consequently, religious beliefs must be qualified.

Second argument: (1) If our religious beliefs are qualified then they become non-assertive (falsifiability criterion). (2) Religious beliefs must be qualified (conclusion of first argument). (3) Therefore, religious statements are non-assertive.

Third argument: (1) If a statement is non-assertative but significant, then it expresses a *blik* (parable of the lunatic). (2) Religious statements are non-assertive and significant (from the conclusion of second argument and the fact that religious beliefs make a difference in our lives). (3) Therefore, religious statements are *bliks*.

This seems to me to be as brief a statement of Hare's argument as can be made while incorporating all of the major points in his essay. When the argument is put forward in this simple form, I think the faults of the argument are particularly obvious. Let us consider some of the more obvious problems.

The first premise of the first argument, that the conclusion of the classical arguments for the existence of God is false if it is not qualified, is the key to the whole argument. This premise exemplifies my contention that the problem of religious knowledge, for those who accept Hare's arguments, is that there is none. I have tried to point out that Hare, like most contemporary philosophers, believes that Hume has carried the day over the classical arguments for the existence of God. Thus, the conclusion of the classical arguments, that God exists, is not merely a statement that has not been proved, but is a false statement. It is false to point out but one problem, because the existence of an infinitely perfect being is incompatible with the existence of evil in the world. Now from the observation that no one has ever solved these problems and that no one has proven God's existence, Hare jumps to this position: we will have to qualify religious assertions so as to remove this incompatibility. But there are other alternatives open. One would be to give up religion, and Hare prefers not to do this. Another would be to continue, in our theologies, to work with these problems, and possibly change our concept of God so as to remove these problems. Certainly this cannot be ruled out on the ground that no one has as yet succeeded in such an endeavor. What I am trying to point out is that Hare has given up any hope of theology as a justification of religious beliefs because it has failed. But it does not follow from the failure of classical theology that religious statements are neither true nor false. All that seems to follow is that they are either unproved, or, with regard to certain conceptions of God's nature, false. The jump to the non-cognitive character of religious utterances, I am arguing, is not warranted. We do not prove they are non-cognitive by means of the falsifiability criterion. For the falsifiability criterion only says that assertions can be qualified to death. Hare is willing to qualify them to death. He is willing to do this, I have tried to show, because they are either false or unproven, and it would make no sense to utter them if either were the case.

I have tried to illustrate that the problem of religious knowledge in contemporary philosophical analysis is that there is none. Now I would like to show how this is related to my claim that the problem of religious language is that of finding a reason for making religious statements. Now Hare does not want to give up religion, for it makes a difference in his life. This brings us, then, to the first premise of the third argument: "If a statement is non-assertive but significant then it expresses a *blik*." Hare illustrates this by means of the "parable of the lunatic." Let us look more closely at this parable. Hare argues that the student has a *blik* about dons; that they want to kill him. Now the reason he calls this a *blik* is because the student allows nothing to count against his belief. His theory, that the dons are out to kill him, according to the falsifiability criterion, is non-assertive.

It would seem, from this statement, that the essential characteristic of a *blik* is that nothing counts against the *blik*; it denies nothing. But the *blik* is still significant, and it is a difference in our own *bliks* and the student's *blik* that gives rise to our different responses to the dons. This seems very peculiar. The student's belief is that the dons are out to kill him. And nothing will falsify this belief, so Hare calls it a *blik*. Then he adds, "It is important to realize we have a sane [*blik*], not no *blik* at all; for there must be two sides to any argument—if he has a wrong *blik,* then those who are right about dons must have a right one."[5] Now there is problem enough in distinguishing right from wrong *bliks* if *bliks* are non-assertive. But the problem I want to point out seems even more fundamental. For if the student has a *blik* that the dons are out to kill him, then my belief that they are not out to kill him, on Hare's argument, is also a *blik*. And "a *blik* does not consist in an assertion or system of them . . . ,"[6] Hare contends. This being the case, my belief that the dons are not out to kill the students is also not assertive. But surely this is false. For if I were to see a group of dons, heavily armed and chasing the lunatic student, I would certainly consider this as evidence against my belief. Hare's position is such that where any person holds a belief and he will allow no evidence to count against it, then this belief, and the negation of this belief are both non-assertive and surely this is false.

Let us call a spade a spade. What makes the student a lunatic is just the fact that nothing counts against his belief. He is not interested in evidence or the facts of the matter. If you want to call this a *blik*, be sure and remember that *bliks* are things lunatics have, and not things sane people have. What the "parable of the lunatic" points out with regard to the problems of religion seems to me to be obvious. Some religious people, and Hare would be wrong to say this of all religious people, will not allow anything to cast doubt on their beliefs. But we don't say these people have *bliks*; we say they are dogmatic and will not engage in honest discussion about their convictions. I can make no other sense out of the notion of *blik*. And I think it is significant the way this interpretation fits in with Flew's example of the two explorers and the invisible gardener. The explorer who believes there is a gardener is totally unjustified in his belief. This doesn't mean his belief is false, but he has no reason to hold it as true. The constant qualifications of his contention that a gardener tends the garden do weaken his claim. And he has failed to explain, by his hypothesis of the gardener, how the garden came to be and grew so well. The non-believer has not explained the presence of the garden either, but he differs from the believer in that he does not have a hypothesis that he will give up under no circumstances. He is at least not dogmatic in his belief that there is no gardener—for he can tell you the conditions that would disprove the statement "there is no gardener." All you have to do is show him the gardener, that care was taken in the garden and it was not an accident. His statement is assertive; it is either true or false. The explorers differ not in their respective *bliks*, as Hare would have it, but in that one of them has a belief he will not give up, and, what is more important, he has a belief that seems to make no sense, for whatever he is talking about in explaining the presence of the garden seems to be nothing like what we mean by "gardener." The other explorer does not have a different *blik*, but he just has no belief about the gardener that he can make sense out of. Let us hope that religious beliefs are not like those of the believing explorer—for they are then only dogmatic utterances of those who refuse to admit they might be wrong.

Let us now draw some general conclusions about the problem of religious knowledge and language. We started with a statement of the falsifiability criterion. It was claimed that a statement that denies nothing asserts nothing. It has been argued by Professors Clarke and Harrison that the statement "God exists" both denies nothing, that is, is compatible with any state of affairs, and yet asserts something, just as tautologies are assertions about necessary states of affairs. Thus "God exists" is necessarily true. Let us grant that necessary statements do *assert* necessary states of affairs. And let us grant that "God exists" is necessarily true. Then the statement "God exists" is compatible with the occurrence of any state of affairs. Then, the statement "God exists" is really like the statement "it is either raining or it is not raining." Both would be true and both are compatible with any state of affairs, for both deny nothing. It seems equally important, however, that while both may be assertive, both are *insignificant*. If, in reply to my question "should I take an umbrella to the game," my companion were to reply "it is either going to rain or it is not going to rain," I should not feel obliged to thank him for this unimportant bit of information. I should not have my plans affected by such a reply, and would still not know what to do. If God's existence is compatible with any state of affairs, then the fact that He exists is of little or no concern to mortals, for we shall have no cause to alter our plans in light of the truth of the necessary statement "God exists." In answer to the question "how should I live my life?," I would find the reply "well, there is a God, you know" of little significance if this statement were like "it is either raining or it is not raining."

Most religious people do consider their beliefs incompatible with the occurrence of certain events. What else could Hare mean when he says that religious beliefs make a difference than that they exclude the possibility of life being meaningless, of all your actions being fruitless, and of the triumph of evil over good. Hare himself points out that he really never knows what the atheists believe, and he thinks "they have never got into the frame of mind of one who suffers from the doubts to which religion is an answer."[7] But if religion answers some doubts, then isn't this to say that one need not entertain certain hypotheses, for they cannot be true. But they cannot be true only if "God exists" is *true and not an insignificant statement*. From this I would lay down as two requirements of religious statements that (1) statements like "God exists" and "God loves us" be assertive, i.e., either true or false, and (2) that these statements be significant, i.e., they deny the possibility of certain other statements being true.

These two requirements are really no more than a reaffirmation of the falsifiability criterion. But I have added something. I have tried to exclude the possibility of religious statements being non-assertive and significant. I have argued that if they are qualified to death, and thus are non-assertive, then they are also not significant. I have tried to point out how Hare gets into problems when he considers religious statements as non-assertive and still holds they make a difference in the way we act. It is not that the statements are non-assertive, but rather that the person making them is dogmatic or that he does not recognize that certain events are incompatible with his beliefs. His beliefs really are incompatible with the truth of other beliefs and he either fails to see it or he will not admit it. On the other hand, I have argued that if we consider these statements as assertive but also necessary truths, then we again are confronted with the problem of their insignificance, for they are compatible with any possible state of affairs. My first point, then, is that religious statements must be both assertive and significant, and consequently certain events in the world should count for or against their truth.

The second point I want to make about religious discourse is that any attempt to say that religious statements are non-assertive moves from the observation that there is no religious knowledge to the assumption that there can be none. And this seems to be an unwarranted assumption. Even in light of thousands of years of religious controversy, I would call this a hasty generalization. Those who claim that religious statements are really expression of *bliks,* or discernment-commitment situations, or confessions, or convictions, or presuppositions, or emotions, or attitudes are *recommending* a particular way of viewing religious language and not, as most claim, describing the logic of religious discourse. What is more, and I have chosen Hare as an example, those who make these recommendations that religious language be viewed differently from descriptive discourse do so in the conviction that if religious statements are not so viewed, they will be either qualified to death or they are false. But such recommendations do not give religious discourse a logic different from the one it does have. And the one it does have, I have argued, is that religious statements are assertive, either true or false, and significant, not compatible with the existence of certain states of affairs.

I can only conclude, as a result of these observations and arguments, that the linguistic analysis of religious language, in the tradition of those like Hare, has failed to do any more than confuse the whole discussion about religious beliefs. They have confused us because they have claimed that religious statements, while they look like statements of fact, are not really statements of fact at all. But, I have argued, there is no way to say their logic is different from descriptive discourse. These philosophers have recommended a way of looking at religious statements, and with this I have no objections. But what I do object to, and I have used Hare as an example, is the contention that these non-assertive statements are still significant in the sense of answering certain *doubts*. For if they are significant in this sense, then I fail to see how they can be compatible with any state of affairs and thus be non-assertive. To be significant in our lives and to affect our attitudes towards the world as well as our actions, it would seem that such statements would have to be assertive. The confusion that the linguistic analysis of religious language perpetrates is that it claims of religious discourse that it is not subject to the canons of descriptive discourse, but then it also claims that religious statements should have a significance in our lives, not only equal to but even greater than those statements of belief that we hold to be true on the basis of the evidence at our command.

Notes

1. Antony Flew, "Theology and Falsification," in *New Essays in Philosophical Theology*, eds. A. Flew and Alasdair MacIntyre (London: SCM Press, 1955), p. 99.

2. R. M. Hare, "Theology and Falsification," in *New Essays in Philosophical Theology*, ed. Flew and MacIntyre, p. 101.

3. Ibid., pp. 99–100.

4. Ibid., p. 100.

5. Ibid.

6. Ibid.

7. Ibid., p. 102.

INDEX